The Abingdon
Children's Sermon Library

Volume 2

The Abingdon Children's Sermon Library

Volume 2

Edited by
Brant D. Baker

Abingdon Press
Nashville

THE ABINGDON CHILDREN'S SERMON LIBRARY
VOLUME 2

Copyright © 2007 by Abingdon Press

This book is printed on acid-free paper.

Library of Congress Cataloging-in-Publication Data

The Abingdon children's sermon library / edited by Brant D. Baker.
    p. cm.
    Includes index.
    (pbk. : alk. paper)
    1. Children's sermons.   2. Sermons, American.   I. Baker, Brant D., 1958-

    BV4315.A25 2006
    252'.53—dc22

                                                                    2005026092

ISBN 978-0-687-33397-4 (vol. 2)
ISBN 0-687-49730-2 (vol. 1)

The sermons entitled "Parting the Red Sea," "Gospel Changes," "The Body of Christ," and "Where Is God?" first appeared in *Let the Children Come,* by Brant D. Baker. Used by permission.

07 08 09 10 11 12 13 14 15 16—10 9 8 7 6 5 4 3 2 1

MANUFACTURED IN THE UNITED STATES OF AMERICA

Contents

Contents

Contents

Contents

Introduction

Not long ago I was struggling through a children's sermon on Sunday when suddenly it hit me: I'm now doing children's sermons with the youngest group of children I've ever had to work with. The age of the children who "come forward" for children's sermons in the church I serve has steadily gone down and now averages around four years old.

Working with children this young requires a different way of thinking and a different kind of planning. Psychosocial development theorist Erik Erikson would remind us that two- to six-year-olds want to explore their world as actively as possible (*Identity: Youth and Crisis* [New York: W.W. Norton & Company, 1968], 115-28). Movement is a more likely reality than sitting still and listening. Instructions need to be more basic; answers to questions aren't likely to be as forthcoming; requested movements or other responses may take more explanation to achieve.

Seven- to twelve-year-olds, on the other hand, are more accustomed to following instructions, giving responses, and sitting still. Children in this "age of industry" like working together to create things and understand a little better how to "make believe." As in Volume 1, we have included some possible responses to aid the flow of actions and stories. The thoughtful leader will want to understand the primary ages of the children and modify these sermons according to their needs.

Noteworthy in this year's *Library* are two special sermon series. In honor of February as "the month of love," we bring you three sermons on that important topic. An even longer series is included for the Lent–Easter season. Based on a fitness theme, it is entitled "Building Up the Body of Christ." This series of seven sermons could be easily adapted for an all-church focus, and the authors have provided plenty of ideas to take the theme as far as you care to (see the series introduction on page 21).

To our new readers, welcome! I believe this second volume of children's sermons continues the high standard for interactive children's learning events we set in Volume 1. Several favorite authors are back, and several new authors have been added. Each brings the benefit of creativity and experience in communicating God's love to children. I hope you enjoy another year of great fun with children, as together we share the life, love, and laughter of our Lord Jesus Christ!

—Brant D. Baker, Editor

Sing to the Lord a New Song

Scripture: Isaiah 42:9-10a; Psalm 96:1-4a

Season/Sunday: New Year's.

Focus: As the old has passed and a new year rolls in, things and people are different. Although we change, God does not, and we continue to praise and worship our unchanging God with a new song.

Experience: The children will look at some old pictures and notice the changes that have occurred. The time will end with a call and response using excerpts from Psalm 96.

Arrangements: You will need enlarged old photographs of the church community (for example, pictures of some of the children, youth, and adults in the church, photos of the church building, or photos of the community). These pictures can be passed around (or projected if the church has the technology). You will need a set of noisemakers such as tambourines, triangles, drumsticks, and shakers (or any noisemakers you use for New Year's). Optional: a helper to distribute noisemakers and help with the call and response.

Leader: Happy New Year, everyone!

Children: Happy New Year!

L: I love the New Year because I look forward to all the new and exciting things to come. I am always reminded of what our prophet Isaiah said, "See, the former things have come to pass, and new things I now declare; before they spring forth, I tell you of them." Well, right before the new year, I decided to clean out some of the old stuff and guess what I found?

C: Candy?

L: No.... I found some old pictures of... (*Fill in with whatever you decide to show and pass the pictures*

1

around. If you have old pictures of people, you
might play a guessing game of who the children
think is in the picture.)

C: Ooooh!

L: I love looking at old pictures. It shows how much
has changed around us. We grow taller. We grow
stronger. We go to a new grade in school and learn
more. Each year there is something new just like
Isaiah said. But you know who doesn't change?

C: I won't!

L: God's love for us will never change. God will always
love us. And because of that we sing to the Lord a
new song, a song of praise and worship using our
new bodies, our new minds, and our new hearts and
souls. Are you ready to do that?

C: Yeah!

L: I am going to pass out some musical instruments.
When you get your instruments, please do not play
with them until I give the sign to do so. I may not
have enough for everyone, so you can share or better
yet, you can make your own joyful noise by clapping, stomping, and snapping (*distribute*
instruments).

L: OK, when I point to you, then you can play the
instrument. But when I hold my palm out (*like*
"stop"), that means stop. Let's test that out. (*Do this*
music-conductor test a couple of times, so that the
children understand the procedure.)

L: Wow! You are a wonderful orchestra. But we're also
going to be a choir, and every time I point, you will
also say "Sing to the LORD a new song!" Let's practice those words.

C: Sing to the LORD a new song.

L: Wonderful, now let's do that with the musical instruments. Remember, when I point to you, you say
those words and play your instrument, and when I
hold my palm up, you stop. Ready, here we go!
(*With palm up*) O sing to the LORD a new song
(*point to the children*).

C: (*Children start playing their instruments and echo*)

Sing to the LORD a new song.

L: (*Hold up palm, indicating no playing*) Sing to the LORD, all the earth, (*point to children*).

C: (*Children play instruments and say refrain*) Sing to the LORD a new song!

L: (*Palm up to stop playing*) Sing to the LORD, bless his name (*point to children*).

C: (*Children play instruments and say refrain*) Sing to the LORD a new song!

L: (*Palm up*) Tell of his salvation, from day to day (*point*).

C: (*Play and say*) Sing to the LORD a new song!

L: (*Palm up*) Declare his glory among the nations (*point*).

C: (*Play and say*) Sing to the LORD a new song!

L: (*Palm up*) His marvelous works among all the peoples (point).

C: (*Play and say*) Sing to the LORD a new song!

L: (*Palm up*) For great is the LORD, and greatly to be praised (*point*).

C: (*Play and say*) Sing to the LORD a new song!

L: Children, that was a beautiful new song we did. Let us close our time with a prayer... (*prayer*).

Joyce S. Fong

Following God's Directions

Scripture: Isaiah 30:21

Season/Sunday: Any, but might work well near New Year's.

Focus: This sermon focuses on following God.

Experience: The children will walk around the sanctuary, stopping occasionally to receive direction and assurance.

Arrangements: This sermon relies on the congregation reading the key verse in unison. This could be accomplished through a projection system, through a common pew Bible available to all, or by printing the verse in the bulletin. The "intersections" referred to below are places in the sanctuary where two or more aisles intersect and a decision has to be made about which way to go.

Leader: Good morning! We're still celebrating a brand new year, and I want to ask you a brand new question: Would you like to practice following God today?

Children: Sure. OK.

L: And maybe if we practice following God today, then we can make this entire year a year in which we follow God! Let's listen to a Scripture verse that tells us about following God. It's Isaiah 30:21.
Congregation, I want you to help us hear the voice of God in this verse from Isaiah, so let's all read aloud together:

Congregation: "Whether you turn to the right or to the left, your ears will hear a voice behind you, saying, 'This is the way; walk in it' " (NIV).

L: Let's all stand up and get in line. We are going to practice following God by listening to these words while we take a little walk. Everybody ready? OK, let's go this direction *(leader starts walking to first "intersection")*. Oh my! Which way should we turn?

4

Let's listen to God's voice as the congregation says
...

Congregation: "Whether you turn to the right or to the left,
your ears will hear a voice behind you, saying, 'This
is the way; walk in it.' "

L: Good. All right then, let's turn to the left *(turn and
continue walking)*. This is kind of exciting, isn't it,
because we don't really know where we will end up!
(Stop at next "intersection.") Here's another intersection, let's listen again for God's voice in God's
word...

Congregation: "Whether you turn to the right or to the left,
your ears will hear a voice behind you, saying, 'This
is the way; walk in it.' "

L: OK, let's turn left again..." *(continue journey)*. Isn't
it good to know that no matter which way we turn,
we can count on God's voice to guide us. Can you
think of other ways we hear God's voice?

C: The Bible. Prayer. Our teachers.

L: Those are all really good answers! OK, here's our
last crossroad. Let's listen one more time...

Congregation: "Whether you turn to the right or to the left,
your ears will hear a voice behind you, saying, 'This
is the way; walk in it.' "

L: *(Make a last turn so that you are heading back to
the front of the sanctuary.)* Wow! You are all good
followers. Let's have a prayer and ask God to help
us to listen all year as we seek to follow our
Lord... *(prayer)*.

Bob Sharman

Letting Our Light Shine

Scripture: Matthew 5:14-16

Season/Sunday: Any Sunday, although the season of Epiphany when God's light to the world is celebrated, would be most appropriate.

Focus: As God's children we are the light of the world.

Experience: The children will affirm that *they* are the light of the world in both word and actions.

Arrangements: None are needed, although you may want to ask the church musician to be prepared to play "This Little Light of Mine" at the close of the children's sermon.

Leader: Jesus loved to teach. And one way Jesus taught was by taking common things that we use around the house to teach a lesson. One time Jesus used the idea of a lamp or a candle to talk about light. He said, "You, my followers, are the light of the world." Can you believe that? We are the light of the world! Let's all say that together,

L & Children: We are the Light of the World!

L: How could we act like a lamp or a candle right now? Maybe we could put our hands on top of our heads to be like flames *(demonstrate)*.

Children: *(Copy action.)*

L: Or maybe we could pretend to be an old-fashioned lantern. Those old lanterns had a candle inside and then something like little doors or shutters that opened and closed to let out more or less light. Maybe we could put our hands at the sides of our faces like a pair of doors or some shutters that open or close over our face *(demonstrate)*.

C: *(Copy action.)*

L: I like that one because Jesus seems to say that we

6

have a choice about whether or not we let our light shine. Jesus said, "No one hides a light under a basket, but places the light where all can see." Don't keep your lantern doors closed *(shut "doors" over face)*, Jesus is saying, but open up *(open "doors")* and let your light shine because we are the Light of the World! Let's all say it together again.

C: We are the Light of the World!

L: *(For each phrase shut "doors" briefly and then open, encouraging children to copy.)* We can help others around us see Jesus, because

C: We are the Light of the World!

L: We do good deeds for those around us, because

C: We are the Light of the World!

L: We show our love by the way we live, because

C: We are the Light of the World!

L: We honor God when we do what is right, because

C: We are the Light of the World!

L: We share our joy when we sing, because

C: We are the Light of the World!

L: That was wonderful! For our closing prayer let's sing "This Little Light of Mine" and invite the congregation to join us . . . *(song)*.

Randy Hammer

Where Is God?

Scripture: Psalm 139:7-12

Season/Sunday: Any.

Focus: One of our beliefs is in God's omnipresence. While this is an abstract concept beyond the capabilities of most of our children, the focus of this sermon is to have fun with it and plant the seeds for later understanding.

Experience: To search the inside of the church for God!

Arrangements: None are needed.

> **Leader:** Good to see everyone today! I have a question to ask: Where is God?
>
> **Children:** Up in the sky.
>
> **L:** Up in the sky. Anywhere else? Is God here?
>
> **C:** Yes. God is everywhere!
>
> **L:** If God is everywhere, then God is here too, right? Where?
>
> **C:** Here!
>
> **L:** Where?
>
> **C:** Here!
>
> **L:** Well, let's look and see if we can find out where God is here. Why don't some of us go look out in the pews, some of us need to go look in the choir, some might come up here. Maybe God is in the pulpit. *(Be sure to look in and around the pulpit, to help demystify that great bulk of furniture!)* Oh, maybe we will find God in the baptismal font; let's look in there. What do you think?
>
> **C:** Too small.
>
> **L:** Too small. OK, how about under the chairs over there? *(To children at back of sanctuary)* Did you find God back there? No? Did anybody check the

choir . . . they look suspicious; better check 'em out. Somebody check over there underneath the piano, would you? Not there either? Well, OK, everybody come on back here. We'll just have to sit down again and think about this. We can't find God or see God, but we know God is here. So, where is God?

C: I know where God is . . . God is everywhere and invisible.

L: God is everywhere and invisible? I wish you'd said that earlier! My, you are clever! That's exactly right. God is here with us, but not only just here but everywhere, all the time, and that makes God pretty amazing.

C: God's beside you.

L: That's right! Well, let's talk to God and thank God for being beside all of us and everywhere . . . *(prayer).*

Brant D. Baker

The Church Puzzle

Scripture: 1 Corinthians 12:14-26

Season/Sunday: Any.

Focus: Church is not about how we fit in, but how we fit together.

Experience: To learn something about being part of the Body of Christ.

Arrangements: You will need a large-piece jigsaw puzzle. A 24-piece puzzle is a good size.

Leader: Good morning! Raise your hand if you have ever put together a puzzle. *(Most all the children will raise their hands.)* Good, because I need your help. *(Pull out the puzzle.)* I just got this—my very first puzzle, and I wonder if you'd help me put it together?

Children: Sure!

L: *(Open lid and look inside, pull out a couple of pieces and look at them.)* Oh, I see, they all fit in this box. *(Put the pieces back in.)* Well, that was easier than I thought; all the pieces are already together.

C: No, you have to put the pieces together.

L: *(Surprised)* You mean they don't just go in the box?

C: No, you put them together.

L: *(Take two pieces out again.)* OK, so you take two pieces and put them together *(force the two pieces together so it is obvious they are not a match)*. Like this?

C: No, that piece doesn't go with that one. They have to fit together.

L: *(Looking at the pieces)* You're right; these two pieces don't fit together. I guess we won't need them *(toss puzzle pieces over your shoulder and reach in the box for two more)*.

C: No, don't throw them away. They go with the puzzle.

L: *(Retrieve the pieces)* Oh, OK. So we need every piece.

C: Find the pieces that fit together.

L: OK, so somehow all the pieces in this box fit together.

C: Yes. Now do you get it?

L: *(Find two pieces that fit together)* Like this?

C: Yeah.... Is this really your first puzzle?

L: *(Smiling)* No, it's not, I was just pretending. But we can learn something about church from putting together a puzzle. We are all like pieces of a puzzle *(hold up a piece)*. Each one of us is unique and special; all of us are children of God, belonging to the church. And when we come to church, our main concern shouldn't be how we fit in, but how we fit together. We all fit together in some unique and special way. When we do, we make up the Body of Jesus Christ. Should I throw away any one piece *(hold up a piece of the puzzle)*?

C: No, you'll need it!

L: That's right, each and every piece is one of us, and each and every piece is needed. Each one of us is important to the Body of Christ, and each one of us is special, and we all fit together in a special way. Let's pray... *(prayer)*.

Jeff Hutcheson

Jesus Is the Bread of Life

Scripture: Matthew 15:32-39

Season/Sunday: Any, but a Sunday when Holy Communion is being served would be most appropriate.

Focus: Jesus as the Bread of Life, the One who satisfies the hunger inside us.

Experience: As the children distribute the "bread and fish," they will be made to feel like Jesus' disciples, as well as be given a taste of service.

Arrangements: Beforehand secure enough small, inexpensive baskets so that each child will have one. Also secure a sufficient number of fish-shaped crackers so that every worshiper can take one. (Have a good supply to spare—you don't want to run out of food while reenacting this miracle story!) Divide the fish-shaped crackers into the baskets. If the church is large, or the children particularly young, it might be a good idea to have adult ushers ready to help in the logistics of the distribution. Finally, as the children distribute the baskets of fish-shaped crackers, an appropriate hymn such as "Break Thou the Bread of Life" may be played (or sung).

> **Leader:** Good morning! Have you ever been away from home, perhaps shopping at the mall or watching a parade or on a fishing trip, or maybe even at church, when you got really hungry?
>
> **Children:** Yes!
>
> **L:** Most of us have done that. Well, often when Jesus was teaching the people, they would walk for miles to hear him teach and time would get away from them so that before long they realized they were hungry and had not brought anything to eat. Jesus felt sorry for the people and did what he could to feed them. In one of those stories the writer of

Matthew's Gospel tells about a crowd of people who had been with Jesus three days and had nothing left to eat. Matthew wants to teach us in this story that Jesus is the Bread of Life. Can you say that with me?

L & C: Jesus is the Bread of Life!

L: Jesus' disciples were able to come up with seven loaves of bread and a few small fish. Who is Jesus?

C: Jesus is the Bread of Life!

L: By breaking and breaking and breaking the seven loaves and few fish into smaller and smaller pieces, Jesus was able to see that all the people were given something to eat. Who is Jesus?

C: Jesus is the Bread of Life!

L: Then the disciples gave the bread and the fish to all the people. And today you get to be Jesus' disciples too! Can you make sure that everyone here this morning gets a piece of bread, because . . .

C: Jesus is the Bread of Life!

L: *(Begin distributing baskets and sending children out for the distribution while you continue talking.)* You may notice that our bread today *(hold up a fish-shaped cracker)* is in the form of a fish. It is thought that the fish was the earliest Christian symbol that was used by Christians to let others know they were followers of Jesus, and let's all say it together *(inviting congregation as well)*, because . . .

C & Congregation: Jesus is the Bread of Life!

L: *(As the distribution is winding down)* After feeding all the people, the disciples brought the baskets back *(signal children to return)*. The disciples saw that they had leftovers! Because . . .

All: Jesus is the Bread of Life!

L: The early followers of Jesus saw in this miracle a spiritual lesson: Jesus satisfies the spiritual hunger and spiritual searching that is inside every one of us. Because . . .

All: Jesus is the Bread of Life!

L: All of us have an inner hunger, a hunger of the heart, to know God, to learn God's ways, to live like God wants us to live. And Jesus is the One who satisfies that hunger, as he shows us who God is, teaches us God's ways, and instructs us on how to best live our lives. Because...

All: Jesus is the Bread of Life!

L: *(Make this refrain the closing prayer by simply adding, "Amen!" or offer closing prayer.)*

Randy Hammer

A Love Letter

Scripture: Galatians 6:11

Season/Sunday: Any, but near Valentine's Day would be appropriate.

Focus: This sermon focuses on how we can express our love in the written word.

Experience: Children will sign their names to a large, heart-shaped letter that will be sent to someone in the congregation who needs a bit of extra love. Consider someone on your prayer list who is ill, injured, or shut-in.

Arrangements: Cut a large heart from poster board or craft paper. On the heart write a simple greeting such as: "Dear _____, We hope that you will get well soon. We are sending you our love in this letter. Love..." The children will each sign their names to the heart. You will need a dark marker or crayon. If you have just a few children, they can sign the letter right away. To save time have them sign only their first names. If you have a larger group, arrange to have the children sign their names later by sending the letter along with them to Sunday school or Children's Church, or having the letter available after the worship service.

Leader:	Have you ever received a letter?
Children:	Yes! I got a letter from my grandma. My friend sent me a letter. I got a letter from my Sunday school teacher.
L:	How do you feel when you receive a letter?
C:	Happy. Surprised. I think it's fun!
L:	Have you ever written a letter?
C:	We wrote them at school. I sent my dad a letter when he was in Iraq.
L:	*(Holding up a Bible)* In the New Testament, we can read many of the letters of the apostle Paul. Paul was

a great Christian missionary who traveled to many places telling people about Jesus. He also wrote lots of letters to churches and to individuals. Some of those letters are now printed in the Bible. *(Show the children one of Paul's letters in the New Testament.)* In one letter Paul wrote, "See what large letters I make when I am writing in my own hand!" We can't see what Paul's handwriting looked like since we don't have any of his original letters, but it's fun to think about him writing these letters to send his love. Today I thought we could send a letter of love to someone in our church. *(Hold up the heart. Have the children read along with you.)* This is a letter for *(say a word about the person who will be receiving the letter).* Since this letter is from all of us, I want each of you to sign your name in your best writing. And then *(person's name)* will be able to see what your handwriting looks like. But first let's say a prayer for *(person's name)* who will be receiving our love letter...*(prayer).*

(Have the children sign their names or announce the plan for doing this. Deliver the letter as soon as possible.)

Barbara Younger

Love with All Your Heart, Soul, and Mind

Scripture: Matthew 22:34-40

Season/Sunday: Any, but around Valentine's Day would be appropriate.

Focus: The children will learn the greatest commandments based on the Gospel of Matthew. The greatest commandment is to "love the Lord your God with all your heart, and with all your soul, and with all your mind." The second commandment is to "love your neighbor as yourself."

Experience: The children will listen to two stories. The first story is about how much a father loves his son. The second story is based on Matthew 22:34-40. For the second story, the children will do motions with their hands. They will end up hugging the person next to them.

Arrangements: It will be helpful to seat the children about half-arm lengths from each other to allow fluid motion.

> **Leader:** Good morning! Today is a special day because we are going to talk about love. How much do you love your toys?
>
> **Children:** A lot!
>
> **L:** How much do you love the people in your families—parents or grandparents, aunts and uncles?
>
> **C:** A lot!
>
> **L:** How much do you love God?
>
> **C:** A lot!
>
> **L:** How much do you think God loves us?
>
> **C:** A lot!
>
> **L:** Show me how much.
>
> **C:** (*Use various hand motions to show how much.*)
>
> **L:** Once, while a father and his son were walking home, the father asked his son, "Do you know how much I love you?" His son said, "This much?" (*Hold out*

17

your hands about six inches apart.) His father shook his head and said, "Nope!" His son tried again and said, "This much?" (*Spread your hands a little wider.*) Again the father said, "Nope." So his son kept on asking, "this much?" several more times, each time spreading his hands wider and wider (*as you say this, spread your hands wider and wider*), until his son's arms were wide open like this (*spread out your arms from side to side and your body should be in the shape of a cross*). Then his father said, "Yes, I love you that much." And his father picked his son up, put him on his shoulder, and continued to walk home.

And do you know what? That's how much God loves us. This much (*spread out your arms from side to side*)! If God loves us this much, then how much should we love God?

C: (*Spread out their arms.*)

L: Yes! Now you are going to help me tell this story. Are you ready?

C: Yes.

L: A long time ago, when Jesus was teaching people about God, a group of people called Pharisees challenged Jesus with hard questions. One of them asked him, "Teacher, which commandment in the law is the greatest?" Children, here's where you can help me. Follow my hand motions. Jesus answered the Pharisee, "You shall love the Lord your God with all your heart (*hold up your hands six inches apart*), and with all your soul (*spread your hands wider to about a little wider than body width*), and with all your mind"— now be careful not to hit each other (*spread them out side to side like a cross*). Good, children, now keep your arms up because we're not done with the story. Then Jesus said, "This is the greatest and first commandment. And a second is like it: 'You shall love your neighbor as yourself.'" Now rest your arms on your neighbors' shoulders and let us pray... (*prayer*).

Joyce S. Fong

18

Love One Another

Scripture: John 13:33-35

Season/Sunday: Any, but appropriate near Valentine's Day.

Focus: We share our love with others so that people will know we are followers of Jesus.

Experience: The children will share symbols of God's love with the gathered community and beyond.

Arrangements: During Sunday school or at a special youth gathering prior to this Sunday, have the children make or decorate enough hearts so that they can be passed out in the congregation during the sermon. Have baskets on hand so the children can distribute the hearts during the children's sermon.

Leader: It's great to see you all this morning! Now, I have a question for you. When you look at me, what are some of the things you can see? What do your eyes tell you about who I am, what I look like, and what I do?

Children: Color of eyes and hair. Your height. You are a pastor.

L: That's right! You can tell all the things that you see with your eyes, can't you? But how do we know about the things that we can't see? How do we know about the things that are inside of us? Things like our thoughts and feelings?

C: We can guess.

L: Jesus tells us that he loves us. Is love something you can see? How do you know when somebody loves you?

C: They do nice things for you. They help you.

L: So, it sounds like we know people love us because of their actions, right?

C: Yes!

19

L: Jesus tells us to love one another. Who remembers decorating hearts in Sunday school a few weeks ago (or this morning)?

C: I do!

L: Today we're going to share those hearts with the congregation as a sign of God's love for us and as a sign of our love for each other. Since love is meant to be shared, everybody can hold on to the heart for a while as a reminder of God's love. But then they can think about someone else who needs to know about God's love and pass the hearts on so that person will know God loves him or her. That's how we show people that we are Christians, by sharing God's love with them. Do you think you can do that?

C: Yes!

L: OK. Here's how we will share God's love today. Take these baskets of hearts and give them to people in the congregation. Then come back here for a prayer.

C: *(Children distribute hearts.)*

L: Now that we have shared a symbol of God's love with each other, let's have a prayer thanking God for loving us ... *(prayer)*

Susan M. Lang

Build Up the Body of Christ: A Lent–Easter Sermon Series

Build Up the Body Of Christ is a children's sermon series of spiritual exercises designed to offer training to novices and saints alike who are part of Christ's Body, the church. Each week offers a new regimen of "fitness" activities to help increase congregational and personal strength through the practice of spiritual disciplines such as prayer, study, meditation, and forms of self-sacrificing love.

The leader has the option to have an assistant over the course of this series. The assistant could take the parts marked "Leader" in these sermons, while the usual children's sermon leader could become the spiritual "trainer." Another alternative is to invite the pastor to be the Trainer if he or she is not the children's sermon leader. The Trainer should plan to come each week dressed in workout clothes and ready to lead that week's spiritual exercise. Alternatively, the usual children's sermon leader may simply lead the exercises, but may want to still consider using some simple wardrobe like a sweatband or a towel around the neck.

The series could easily be adapted to a congregation-wide focus that might include a series of adult sermons on the same themes, banners to serve as visual reminders, and a worship center to provide a focus for the topic. The banners or worship center could display items traditionally associated with the spiritual disciplines:

- "Jog Your Prayer Life": a statue of praying hands, prayer books, or beads

- "Hold On to Hope": a communion chalice symbolizing the assurance of eternal life

- "Push Up Spiritual Priorities": a loaf of communion bread signifying forgiveness and Christ's sacrifice

- "Stretch Your Faith": an offering plate

- "Bend an Ear": a Bible

- "Lift Your Cares": a cross

- "Share New Life": a baptismal font or towel and basin

The leader/trainer could add the visuals to the worship display from week to week, using them during each week's review of the previous exercises.

Build Up the Body of Christ: Jog Your Prayer Life

Scripture: Luke 4:1-13

Season/Sunday: First Sunday in Lent.

Focus: Lent as a season to deepen our spiritual priorities by spending time in prayer for ourselves and for others.

Experience: The children will participate in several exercises, primarily jogging in place.

Arrangements: The trainer will need a set of wrist weights and a sufficient number of wristbands or rubber bracelets for each child to take as a reminder.

Leader:	How many of you do exercises? What kinds of exercises do you do?
Children:	*(Various replies)*
L:	Let's do some of those exercises now. Everybody on your feet and stretch!
C:	*(Stretch.)*
L:	Now let's touch our toes!
C:	*(Touch toes.)*
L:	Now let's pretend like we're lifting weights.
C:	*(Pretend to lift weights.)*
L:	Whew, let's rest! Let me ask you this: Why do people take time to exercise?
C:	To lose weight. To get stronger. To get in shape.
L:	Those are all good answers. Exercise helps us be physically healthy, doesn't it? But here's a question: what kinds of exercises can the church do to get spiritually healthy?
C:	Be nice. Read the Bible. Pray.
L:	Wow! Those are good answers too! Well, this Sunday begins a season that we call Lent. For forty days Christians are supposed to be getting ready for the most important Sunday in the church year, Easter. So over the next several weeks we're going to be working on exercises we can do to become

spiritually healthy and build up the Body of Christ.
And just like many professional athletes have physical trainers who help them design exercise programs,
during our Lenten spiritual training program we're
going to have a trainer. And so here with today's
advice on how you can jog your prayer life is Pastor
Bob (or Betty)!

Trainer: *(Perhaps jogging down the aisle, wearing wrist
weights, dabbing sweat on face with towel. If leader
is functioning as trainer, put on wrist weights as you
begin to jog in place).* Good morning! Everybody up!
Let's start jogging in place!

C: *(Children jog in place.)*

T: Sometimes we use the word *jog* to mean run, but
sometimes we use it to mean giving something a
nudge to get it going. Lent is a good time to get going
with our prayer lives. With regular times to pray, we
will begin to feel more spiritually healthy. Joggers
find that they have more energy and endurance, and
pray-ers discover the same kind of inner strength.
OK, let's take a break and have a seat.

C: *(Sit.)*

T: Praying is like spiritual jogging. Healthy Christians
pray to stay spiritually fit. But let me ask you something: did you notice these things around my wrists?
What are they?

C: *(Various replies)*

T: These are wrist weights. Sometimes joggers add some
weight so that they get more of a workout.
(Distribute wristbands or bracelets to each child.)
During Lent our prayer lives can become even more
productive if we remember to add some weight.
These bands can remind us to carry the burdens of
others to God in prayer. We'll get more of a spiritual
workout by adding someone else's burdens, the
things that weigh them down, to our own prayers.

Let's pray together right now. Dear God, thank
you for sending Jesus. Help us remember to pray for
the people we know who are hurt and sad, and for
all of your people each day during Lent. Amen.

Ann Liechty and Phyllis Wezeman

Build Up the Body of Christ: Hold On to Hope

Scripture: Genesis 15:1-12, 17-18

Season/Sunday: Second Sunday in Lent.

Focus: Lent as a time to trust God's promises and to reach for higher levels of faith.

Experience: The children will pretend to climb a rope as a faith-strengthening exercise.

Arrangements: The trainer will need a length of rope for the main activity, and a small section of rope for each child to take as a reminder.

Leader: Welcome to the second Sunday in Lent! During Lent we prepare for Easter by "Building Up the Body of Christ." Last week the spiritual fitness challenge was to "Jog Your Prayer Life!" *(If using a "Trainer," reintroduce that person to lead remainder of sermon.)*

Trainer: Everybody up, let's jog in place!

Children: *(Start jogging.)*

T: Jogging is good for our heart muscle, and praying is good for our spiritual heart *(stop jogging and signal children to do so as well)*. But sometimes we want to strengthen other parts of our bodies as well. Let me see you flex your muscles *(leader demonstrates by striking a bodybuilder pose)*.

C: *(Flex muscles)* I'm strong!

T: You are strong! But remember, if we are to be stronger Christians, we need to do some spiritual strengthening *(take out the rope)*. How could this rope be used for physical training?

C: Jumping. Pulling. Have a tug of war.

T: You have lots of good ideas! I was thinking: what if we could fasten this rope to the ceiling and use it for climbing? That would really strengthen our upper

25

bodies—our arms, chest, and shoulders. Let's pretend that we're climbing a rope to the ceiling. *(Trainer and children pretend, continue talking...)* If we were to climb this rope, we would have to believe that it would hold us, that it wouldn't come crashing down. During Lent, we remind ourselves that God offers us a promise we can trust. From the very beginning, God has made promises to human beings—just like the promise God made to Abraham to bless him and to make his children as numerous as the stars in the heavens. But that promise didn't happen for Abraham right away. He had to keep looking up and believing God and building up his faith—sort of like learning to climb a rope. OK, let's stop climbing and take a rest *(sit)*.

(Distribute sections of rope to each child). We may not make it to the top of the rope for quite awhile, but we can climb higher and higher as we grow stronger. This piece of rope is to help us remember to hold on to the hope we have in God's promises, to climb higher, and to trust in God as Abraham did! Let's have a prayer.... Dear God, thank you that we can trust your promises. Help us to hold on to hope and to reach for the stars. Amen.

Ann Liechty and Phyllis Wezeman

Build Up the Body of Christ: Push Up Spiritual Priorities

Scripture: 1 Corinthians 10:1-13

Season/Sunday: Third Sunday in Lent.

Focus: Repentance provides the leverage to help us push spiritual priorities higher in life.

Experience: The children will have a chance to do push-ups and to be lifted by a lever and fulcrum.

Arrangements: The trainer/leader will need a lever and fulcrum. A flat board and a block of wood or brick could do the job, but be creative with what is already available. The leader/trainer should practice in advance to find the right fulcrum point for one to lift the other, or if the leader is the trainer, practice with a volunteer. The trainer should also have a small rock and a craft stick or tongue depressor for each child to take away as a reminder of the lesson.

As an added twist this week, it might be fun if a soundperson could supply a quick burst of music from the *Rocky* movies.

Leader:	Well, you're all looking more and more healthy! Do you remember that during Lent we're learning how to strengthen our spiritual bodies so that we can be people of strong faith. Everybody up!
Children:	*(stand)*
L:	*(Start jogging in place, indicate children should follow lead.)* Two weeks ago our trainer helped us think about prayer as a way to get a healthier spiritual body *(stop jogging, start climbing)*, and last week we talked about holding on to the rope of hope in God to get stronger. Let's get Pastor Bob (or Betty) back in to help us with today's exercise.
Trainer:	*(Rocky soundtrack)* Good to see you all looking so strong! Can anyone here do a push-up?

C: *(Try to do push-ups)* That's hard!

T: That really is hard, isn't it? And you know what, a spiritual push-up isn't much easier! We can make the Body of Christ stronger when we push up spiritual priorities—that means we should make spiritual concerns like love, joy, and peace more important in our lives. That sounds hard, but I have a secret to make it easier. We can use a "lever" to help us do our spiritual push-ups. With a lever we can push up much more weight than we can lift. A lever is a bar that turns on a fixed point, or fulcrum, like a seesaw *(leader and trainer demonstrate, or solo leader demonstrates with volunteer or a child)*. See *(point to fulcrum)*, this rock (or block of wood) is a fulcrum that makes it easier to push up something too heavy to lift.

C: *(Various children can take turns being lifted with lever. Trainer should always be the person doing the lifting!)*

T: We can use a lever to push up our spiritual priorities, too *(distribute rocks and craft sticks)*. When we do that, the part we push on *(point to stick)*, the lever, is called "repentance," which means we tell God we are sorry for the sin in our lives and ask for help to change. *Repentance* means we quit thinking only of ourselves and our own selfish desires and instead concentrate on loving God and God's people. For this lever of repentance to work, we must add a fulcrum—a place of support *(show children where to place the rock and demonstrate)*. As Christians we offer our repentance to Christ, who is our Rock, our strength, our fulcrum. With Christ as our Rock we are able to push up more spiritual priorities like love, joy, and peace.

Let's have a prayer. . . . Dear God, thank you for the gift of repentance. Help us push up those things that matter most in life—love, joy, and peace. Amen.

Ann Liechty and Phyllis Wezeman

Build Up the Body of Christ: Stretch Your Faith

Scripture: Luke 15:1-3, 11b-32

Season/Sunday: Fourth Sunday in Lent.

Focus: The sermon develops the idea of using what faith we have to help develop even more.

Experience: The children will follow the lead of the trainer in several stretches.

Arrangements: The trainer should think through several basic stretching moves to show the children. The take-away item for this sermon is a rubber band, one for each child.

Leader Can you remember how many Sundays we have been building up the Body of Christ? We began by "Jogging Our Prayer Lives" *(leader and children jog in place)*, then we "Held On to Hope" *(all pretend to climb rope)*, and last week we learned how to "Push Up Spiritual Priorities" *(pretend to push down on a lever)*. So how many weeks have we been preparing for Easter?

Children: Three!

L: Right! So today is the fourth Sunday in Lent. Our next spiritual fitness challenge is to "Stretch Your Faith!" and here to lead us is Pastor Bob (or Betty).

Trainer: Stretching is so important for our muscles *(demonstrate a few stretches and encourage children to follow lead. Be sure to hold each stretch for several counts)*.

C: *(Stretch.)*

T: *(Continue to demonstrate and hold various stretches while talking)* Doesn't that just make you feel better all over? Stretching can be hard at first, but the more we do it, the better we feel! You know, the same is true in our spiritual life. God wants us to stretch in our faith, and when we do, we feel better and end up with even more faith! In the story of the prodigal son, the son treated his father badly. He demanded his inheritance and left home to spend it all unwisely. The father could have given up, lost faith in his son, and forgotten him. But instead, he chose to have faith that his son would one day come home. That's why the father was watching and waiting on the day his son returned. There were surely some days the father wanted to quit believing! And what about the son? It must have been hard for him to admit that he was wrong and to come back to his father. But even though he had sinned, he chose to have faith in his father's mercy. Having faith is like stretching: the more we stretch, the more we are able to stretch the next time.

(Distribute rubber bands) During Lent we are getting ready to have faith in the greatest miracle of all. God challenges us to live our lives with faith that Christ rose from the dead. Once we stretch our faith to believe, then we must stretch even further by telling others the resurrection story of Jesus. These rubber bands can help us remember to stretch our faith. Let's have a prayer...Dear God, thank you for the faith you place in us. Help us stretch to reach out to others in your name. Amen.

Ann Liechty and Phyllis Wezeman

Build Up the Body of Christ: Bend an Ear

Scripture: John 12:1-8

Season/Sunday: Fifth Sunday in Lent.

Focus: Discipline helps us listen for Christ's call.

Experience: The children will bend their own ears, will bend the shape of an ear out of the materials provided, and will listen in silence for God's voice in prayer.

Arrangements: The trainer will need an exercise DVD or videotape (although no player required for this sermon), and a sufficient number of pipe cleaners or Wikki Stix (available at most craft or toy stores) for each participant.

> **Leader:** If we bend right side, backward, left side, forward, and up again, we can count the number of Sundays in Lent since we started bodybuilding *(demonstrate and invite children to participate as leader counts 1, 2, 3, 4, 5).*
>
> **Children:** *(Bend and count.)*
>
> **L:** Good for you! We bent five times—once for each Sunday in Lent, including today. *(If time permits review the exercises and themes.)* Are you ready for our next exercise? Here's Pastor Bob (or Betty)!
>
> **Trainer:** Bending is another good exercise to limber up our bodies and to reduce our waistlines! *(Demonstrate the bending exercise again first without counting and then with counting.)*
>
> **C:** *(Follow lead.)*
>
> **T:** It helps to have someone to count and keep us all together, doesn't it? That's why people sometimes exercise to workout videos like this one. *(Hold the sample videotape or DVD to the ear.)* That's funny, though, I can't hear anyone. Can you? *(Let a few children try "hear" the package.)*

C: It doesn't work that way! You have to put it in a player!

T: Oh, I have to put it into the player to hear someone help me work out? I can't just buy the recording to build up my body, right?

C: Right!

T: Instead I have to listen and do what the instructor says! For our spiritual bodybuilding we need to listen too. Whose voice do we listen for?

C: Jesus! God!

T: Right! And that's our exercise for this Sunday in Lent: we need to "bend an ear" to listen for God's voice *(cup the ear and bend the head as though listening and invite the participants to do the same).* The Bible tells the story of Mary. Mary understood the importance of bending an ear to Jesus. She knew what she needed to do to honor Jesus. She sacrificed an expensive jar of ointment to show Jesus how much she cared, even though other voices around her made fun and scolded. Mary had the reward of hearing Jesus praise her for her loving devotion. Hearing Mary's story reminds us that we must pay attention to our Lord as we prepare to experience Easter.

If we are going to build up the Body of Christ, we need to bend our ears too. *(Trainer should bend a pipe cleaner or Wikki Stix in the shape of an ear. Distribute one to each child to create a "bent" ear.)* What we need to do is bend an ear to listen for God's message. If we begin to listen every day, we will hear the call of Christ.

While we pray, let's all bend our ears and listen. . . . Dear God, thank you for Mary's example of listening, and help us listen too. . . *(pause for a time of silence).* Amen.

Ann Liechty and Phyllis Wezeman

Build Up the Body of Christ: Lift Your Cares

Scripture: Luke 19:28-40

Season/Sunday: Palm/Passion Sunday, the Sixth Sunday in Lent.

Focus: Obedience to God brings us through times of suffering and pain.

Experience: A child will experience the challenge of holding light weights for a long time, other volunteers will experience waving the weights, and all of the children will be invited to wave palms.

Arrangements: The leader/trainer will need a set of very light barbell weights and a palm branch for each participant.

Leader: Good morning! I've got some weights here that aren't very heavy *(show weights)*. Who would be willing to be strong and lift these weights up while we count how many Sundays have passed in the season of Lent?

Children: Me! I will!

L: *(Have a volunteer stretch arms out straight to sides while holding barbells and keep them in place while Leader reviews the first five spiritual exercises. Encourage the "weight lifter" to keep holding up the barbells.)* OK, the first week we jogged our prayer lives *(leader and children jog in place)*, then we held on to hope *(all pretend to climb rope)*, then we learned how to push up our spiritual priorities *(pretend to push down on a lever)*, and then we stretched our faith *(do a stretching exercise)*. And who remembers last week's exercise?

C: To bend an ear!

L: Right, we bent an ear to hear God's voice in prayer *(demonstrate motion for all to copy)*. So how many weeks have we been preparing for Easter?

C: Five!

L: That's right. Today is the sixth and last Sunday in Lent. This Sunday has a special name. Does anyone know what Sunday this is?

C: Palm Sunday.

L: That's right. How are you doing with the weights *(check with "weight lifter" and ask him or her to hold on a little longer)*. Great! Now, let's have Pastor Bob (Betty) come back and tell us about Palm Sunday and give us our exercise for this week.

Trainer: On Palm Sunday Jesus rode into Jerusalem on a donkey while the crowds waved palm branches in the air and shouted, "Hosanna!" which means, "Save us!" *(Demonstrate with palms.)* I'd guess those palm branches were not as heavy as these barbells. Are your arms getting really tired?

Weight Lifter: Yes! *(If the "weight lifter" has been able to hold on this long, celebrate that accomplishment.)*

T: Well, you've done a great job because even holding light weights for a long time can be hard work. You can put them down now. Waving the palm branches on Palm Sunday was a joyful, easy thing to do because the people thought that Jesus was riding into town to save them from their enemies, the Romans. By Thursday, when Jesus didn't behave the way they expected, the crowd was shaking angry fists and crying, "Crucify him!"

When Jesus was crucified, his arms had to hold the weight of his whole body on the cross *(have children stretch out arms)*. We thought it was difficult to hold up these little weights *(point to barbells)*; imagine how much more difficult it was for Jesus! *(Invite children to put arms down.)*

In life, we sometimes act like the people in that crowd. We want everything to work out just the way we imagine it should. We like to celebrate the easy times *(wave palm branch)*. But in life, everyone has difficult times. Would it be as easy to wave these barbells like we wave the palm branches?

C: Yes! No! *(Let a couple of children try to wave barbells.)*

T: You can do it, but do you think you could do it for very long?

C: No!

T: As Christians we know that Jesus understands the hard times of life because he experienced suffering and death. On Palm Sunday, we remember that story, not to make us feel sad, but to remember that Jesus understands our burdens and our cares. Our "weightlifting" exercise reminds us that if we lift our troubles toward heaven, God helps us bear the hard times of life. When we do, we find that God has a plan for us that will bring more joy than anything we could imagine. *(Distribute palm branches.)*

Let's all lift our cares and cry, "Hosanna! God save us!"

C: *(Waving palm branches)* Hosanna! God save us!

T: Let's have a prayer. . . . Dear God, thank you that Jesus was willing to share our burdens. Help us, like him, to turn to you in difficult times. Amen.

Ann Liechty and Phyllis Wezeman

Build Up the Body of Christ: Share New Life!

Scripture: John 20:1-18

Season/Sunday: Easter Sunday.

Focus: The message of Easter awakens us to the promise of new life and the importance of serving others.

Experience: Children will review all of the spiritual exercises learned so far and will pantomime acts of cleansing and service, using a towel.

Arrangements: The leader/trainer will need a white towel to wear around his or her neck and will need a sufficient number of white paper towel sheets for each participant. Option: since it can be difficult to find plain white paper towels, and in view of the special day, leaders may even consider purchasing small white cloth hand towels to distribute to the children.

> **Leader:** *(Have the white towel draped around the neck and use it to mop forehead as though just finished exercising.)* We've spent six weeks getting ready for this day! Do you remember all the things we have done? Let's review: we've jogged our prayer lives *(leader and children jog in place)*, we've held on to hope *(all pretend to climb rope)*, we've learned how to push up our spiritual priorities *(pretend to push down on a lever)*, we've stretched our faith *(do a stretching exercise)*, we've bent an ear *(bend ear)*, and we've lifted the weights of our cares to Jesus *(wave a pretend palm branch)*.
>
> We've spent six weeks building up the Body of Christ *(point to everyone as part of that "body")* so that we're ready for this special day. Who knows what is special about this Sunday?
>
> **Children:** It's Easter! The Easter Bunny came!
>
> **L:** Yes, but there's something even more important than that! Who knows what it is?

C: Jesus rose from the dead.

L: That's right! And our Spiritual Trainer, Pastor Bob (Betty), is going to tell us all about it.

Trainer: Today we share the story of Jesus' resurrection! God raised Jesus to new life. And now we know through faith in Jesus that death is not the end, but the beginning of eternal life.

But now, let me ask you a question: after we have exercised our physical bodies, what do we need to do?

C: Rest. Take a shower.

T: That's right—after physical exercise we need to take a bath or shower *(pantomime taking a shower or bath and drying with towel from around neck)*. Water is important to the Body of Christ too. In the early church, Easter was often the day when new Christians were baptized after spending the forty days of Lent preparing. One of the meanings of baptism is that Christ washes away sin, so we can be clean and ready for our new life as Christians. *(Leader/Trainer distributes towels to children.)* This towel can remind us of the water of baptism that washes us spiritually clean. But the towel symbolizes something more too—it reminds us of service, like the time Jesus served the disciples by washing and drying their feet. The towel has become a symbol of baptized Christians in service to the world *(drape towel over arm like a waiter)*.

After Jesus rose from the dead, he told his followers to go and share the message with others. We haven't spent six weeks developing our spiritual muscles just to show off! We've done it so that we can be ready to spread the good news to other people through our words and in our good deeds of service. The church is the Body of Christ on earth today. Jesus walks and talks, heals and cares through you and me. The message of Easter is that we can be cleansed, forgiven, and restored to new life *(use towel to clean off and invite children to follow lead)*, so we can then use our new lives to serve others *(drape towel over arm again, inviting children to follow lead).*

Congratulations! We've made it through the spiritual exercise program of Lent. Now let's keep this Body of Christ healthy and full of Easter's new life today—and always—by serving God's people! Let's have a prayer...Dear God, thank you for the powerful message of Easter. Make us strong disciples so that we may help others in Christ's name. Amen.

Ann Liechty and Phyllis Wezeman

Give a Cheer!

Scripture: Ephesians 4:4-6

Season/Sunday: Any.

Focus: The sermon focuses on the unity we have in the Body of Christ.

Experience: The children will become cheerleaders, with responsibility to help lead a section of the congregation in a prearranged cheer.

Arrangements: Besides having a copy of the cheer in hand, the leader will want to think through a logical way of dividing the worshiping congregation into four sections. As an alternative, combine parts of the cheer and use fewer sections, or include additional phrases from Ephesians 4 to create more sections ("one faith," "one baptism," and "one hope" are all present in the original text).

Leader: Good morning! I have a question for you: are we all the same?

Children: No!

L: Look out there at the congregation; are they all the same?

C: No!

L: But even though we might all be different, we all have enough in common to say that we are one in the church, and that's something to cheer about! Would you like to help lead a cheer for unity in Jesus Christ?

C: Yes!

L: OK, let's see, how about you three children moving over here in front of this part of the congregation; and when I point at you, you help them shout out as loud as you can, "One God!" Let's give it a try (*practice with children and congregational section*).

That was great! OK, who would like to lead the next section?

C: Me! I will!

L: OK, you two can lead this section *(take children to designated area),* and your cheer is "One Lord!" Remember, when I point to you, you lead them...ready? *(Point to this new section and then surprise the first section by pointing at them...have fun!)* OK, let's take all of you *(indicating next grouping of children)* and have you lead the choir in saying "One Spirit!" I happen to know that the choir needs a lot of help being led, so you've got a big job, are you ready?

C: Yes!

L: OK *(point).* That was great! OK, the last section will be led by all of you *(lead children to appointed area),* and your cheer is "One Body!" Are you ready, here we go *(point).*

C & Section 1: One Body!

L: Wow, that was really great! OK, let's practice a minute *(point at each section in turn, then perhaps mix up the order, pointing randomly at various sections).* All right, I think you're ready, so here we go:

Some of us may be men, some of us may be women, but still... *(point at each section in whatever order desired).*

Some of us may be old, some of us may be young, but still... *(point at each section).*

We may all have different amounts of money, but still... *(point at each section).*

We may all be different shapes and sizes, but still ... *(point at each section).*

We may all be different colors, but still... *(point at each section, perhaps going around a few extra times).*

That was great! And all we need to say after that is "Amen," on three—one, two, three,

All: Amen!

Brant D. Baker

Growing God's Word

Scripture: Mark 4:1-20

Season/Sunday: This would be best in late spring, early summer so that the plants can be transplanted to the garden when they begin to grow and the children can tend them.

Focus: We want to be like the good soil in which the seed is planted so that God's Word can produce a rich harvest in our lives.

Experience: The children will help plant seeds in a variety of soil.

Arrangements: First, you will need four flowerpots. One will be empty, one will be filled with gravel, one will be filled with weeds, and one will be filled with good soil. You may want to consider a drop cloth for the floor to catch spills and/or a small table to work on. Second, you will need a supply of seeds. Large seeds are easier for children to manipulate. Finally, prepare beforehand a sufficient number of sandwich bags with a handful of good soil and a seed packet (mixed together).

> **Leader:** This morning we are going to plant some seeds in different pots and see which ones we think will grow. Who wants to plant the first pot?
>
> **Children:** I do!
>
> **L:** Here is the first pot, now plant the seed in it. What do you see when you plant the seed? Do you think it will grow?
>
> **C:** Hey, the pot is empty! It won't grow in this pot! There's nothing here.
>
> **L:** You're right. In the story we just heard (*or, Jesus tells a story in which . . .*) this pot is like the sower, planting the seed on a path. There is no soil for the seed to grow. It can't grow in just air, can it? What does a seed need to grow?
>
> **C:** Dirt. Water. The sun. Somebody to take care of it.

L: That's right! Now, who wants to plant the second pot?

C: I do!

L: What do you see when you plant this one? Do you think it will grow?

C: The pot is filled with gravel! There's no dirt. It can't grow in this!

L: That's like the seed that falls on rocky ground. It won't grow, will it?

C: No! There's no dirt there.

L: That's right. Who wants to plant the third pot?

C: I do.

L: What do you see when you plant this one? Do you think it will grow?

C: It's filled with weeds! There's no room for the seed!

L: That's right; it might have a chance, but probably not. It's like the seed that was choked by the thorns and couldn't grow. OK, the last pot has some good soil, just like Jesus talked about in the story. Who wants to help plant this seed?

C: I do!

L: Do you think this seed will grow?

C: Yes, if we take care of it.

L: That's right! Jesus tells us that when we listen to God's word and act on it, we'll be like the good soil that receives the seed and helps it grow into beautiful flowers, vegetables, or fruit. Seeds need good soil and water and sun. What else can we do to help the seed of God's word grow in us?

C: That we read the Bible. Come to church and Sunday School. By praying. By inviting friends to church.

L: Those are all great answers! (*Distribute seed and soil packets.*) Here is some good soil and seeds for each of you to take home. Plant the seeds in the soil and take care of them to remind you that Jesus wants us to be like this good soil. Let's share a prayer that we will be good soil for God's word to grow in us . . . (*prayer*).

Susan M. Lang

Planting Seeds/Growing God's Word in Us

Scripture: 1 Corinthians 3:6; Luke 8:11

Season/Sunday: Any.

Focus: The sermon focuses on the importance of God's word in Scripture.

Experience: The children will experience a visual of growing from the inside and practice a couple of foundational verses for growing.

Arrangements: None needed.

> **Leader:** Good Morning everyone! You know you are growing bigger all the time—look at how big you are getting. Look!
>
> **Children:** *(Look at themselves.)*
>
> **L:** Well, our scripture verse for today talks about growing. It comes from 1 Corinthians 3:6. "I planted the seed" says Paul, "...but God made it grow." Wow, a seed has been planted in you! Do you feel like a seed is planted in you?
>
> **C:** Yes. No. What kind of seed?
>
> **L:** Well that was the question I was going to ask, what kind of seed could it be? Do you have a broccoli seed planted in you?
>
> **C:** Yuck! No!
>
> **L:** Well maybe there is an oak tree seed in you, or maybe a beautiful flower seed is inside of you. Everybody open their mouths; let me see if there are any seeds down there.
>
> **C:** *(Children open mouths!)*
>
> **L:** Well, I don't really see any flower or broccoli seeds inside of you, but Jesus once said, "The seed is the word of God" (Luke 8:11 NIV). Hmmm. If the seed is the word of God and God is going to grow that

43

seed, what do you think we ought to do?

C: I don't know. Eat more green beans?

L: Do you think that maybe we should plant "seeds" of God's word into ourselves?

C: Yes!

L: Sure, if we learn God's word it's like putting God's word into ourselves. In fact, let's start right now to put some of God's *word-seeds* inside us, so that God can make them grow. And we can start with the two verses you just heard. I'll say them and you repeat them back. Ready? Here we go, "I planted the seed..."

C: *(Echo.)*

L: "...but God made it grow."

C: *(Echo.)*

L: That was great! Now let's try another one, "The seed is the word of God."

C: *(Echo.)*

L: I think those *word-seeds* from God are growing inside of you already! I want you to practice these seeds again today for your families when you get home so you don't forget them. And let's have a prayer giving thanks for all God's good seeds... *(prayer).*

Optional ending:

L: I think those *word-seeds* from God are growing inside of you already! And I think you are learning them so well that you could teach these *word-seeds* to the congregation. Let's turn around and see if we can teach them. Everybody ready? Repeat after us... *(Leader can prompt children if necessary; children repeat, echoed by congregation.)*

Bob Sharman

Mother, May I?

Scripture: Ephesians 6:1-3

Season/Sunday: Mother's Day (but may be adapted for Father's or Grandparents' Day).

Focus: This sermon focuses on the importance of children obeying and honoring their parents because parents help keep children safe and growing to be God's servants.

Experience: The children will play a version of the game "Mother, May I." One participant (a helper) will ask ridiculous and unsafe "may I" questions, and the leader will say no to the participant to keep him/her safe.

Arrangements: You will need one adult who will ask the ridiculous questions. Prepare beforehand how you want to set up the game and where children will stand. The game is played by placing the children at a distance from the leader (for example, children at the top of the church aisle, the leader at the bottom). The objective is for the children to get to the leader by asking, "Mother, may I" questions such as "Mother, may I walk three steps forward?" The "mother" may respond, "Yes, you may," or "No, you may not." If the leader is not a mother, perhaps someone could be asked to fill this role, while the children's sermon leader becomes the "ridiculous participant."

Leader: Good morning, everyone. Today we are going to play a game called "Mother, may I." *(If you have a lot of children, you may want to select a small group of children who want to play a game.)* Have you played this game before?

Children: Yes! No!

L: Well, let me explain the rules, just in case some of you forgot them. I will stand right here and all of you will stand over there. Your goal is to get to me by asking "Mother, may I" questions. For example,

you can ask, "Mother, may I walk three steps for-
wards?" or "Mother, may I hop three hops to the
right?" Then I will say, "Yes, you may" or "No, you
may not." If I say yes, then you can go. If I say no,
then you have to stay in the same spot. Ready to
play the game?

C: Yes!

L: OK, let's take our places. *(The adult helper joins the
children to play. Select one child to start.)*

C: Mother, may I . . . *(about three children go first and
say yes to all of them).*

Adult Helper: Mother, may I do three cartwheels on the pews?

L: *(With a look of horror)* No, you may not!

C: Mother, may I . . . *(let two more children go before
interruption).*

Adult Helper: *(Interrupts)* Mother, may I eat 50 chocolate chip
cookies?

L: *(With a look of horror)* No, you may not, and it's
not your turn yet!

C: Mother, may I . . . *(let two more children go before
interruption).*

Adult Helper: *(Interrupts)* Mother, may I skip school tomorrow
and play all day?

L: *(With a look of horror)* No, you may not!

C: Mother, may I . . . *(end the game when a child
reaches the leader and gather the children together).*

L: That was a fun game. Now, let's talk about *(Adult
helper name)*. Why do you think I said no to doing
three cartwheels on the pews?

C: Because it's not safe. Because pews are for sitting.

L: That's right! I want to keep you all safe. Now, why
did I say no to eating 50 chocolate chip cookies?

C: Because you get a stomachache if you do that.

L: That's right! I want you all to keep healthy. Now,
why did I say no to skipping school?

C: Because we need to go to school to learn.

L: That's right! I want to make sure that you all get
your education. Did I say no to be mean?

C: No.

L: That's right! I said no in order to help and guide.

Did you know that's what real parents do? Sometimes your parents say no to you just to keep you healthy, safe, and smart. They are always looking out for you and guiding you to be God's children. As children, you should do your best to obey and honor your parents. In Ephesians 6:1-3, it says, "Children, obey your parents in the Lord, for this is right. 'Honor your father and mother'—this is the first commandment with a promise: 'so that it may be well with you and you may live long on the earth.'" Let's have a prayer and thank God for parents... (*prayer*).

Joyce S. Fong

When Sad Things Happen

Scripture: Job 1:1–2:9

Season/Sunday: Any.

Focus: God is with us, even when bad things happen in our lives.

Experience: The children will create a litany that the whole congregation will use.

Arrangements: Have available an easel with a large newsprint pad (or a large piece of poster board) and a marker.

Leader: Good morning! What's the weather like? What kind of day do we have today?

Children: *(Varied responses)*

L: It's a lovely day today; but when it's not such a nice day, we sometimes get crabby. We feel like bad things are happening to us. *(If bad weather: "When we have bad weather, we don't feel that things are going too well for us, do we?")* When are some other times when things aren't going well for us? What are some of the sad things that can happen in our lives? As you mention them, I'm going to write them on this large paper so that we can all see them. *(Write responses, leaving a line at the top to write the response that is suggested below.)*

C: *(Varied responses. Be sure that things like storms, divorce, death, illness, and other serious problems are mentioned.)*

L: These are all sad things, and most of these are things that happen even though we have nothing to do with making them happen. There is a story in the Bible about a man named Job who had some really bad things happen to him. He had lots of animals: oxen, donkeys, sheep, and camels. They were all taken from him or burned up in a fire. His servants who

cared for the animals were killed. His children were
killed when a great wind blew down the house
where they were having a meal together. And then he
got terrible sores all over his body. Now how do you
suppose Job felt then?

C: *(Varied responses)*

L: Job was very upset, but he believed in God so much
that he knew that God was with him in the sad times
as well as the good times.

(Point to the list) We've listed lots of bad things
that happen in our lives, but we can know that God
doesn't cause those bad things to happen specifically
to us. We can know that God is sad when we are
sad, and God is with us even in the sad times.

We're going to use these sad things that happen
in our lives to make a litany, a kind of special prayer.
I will read the list, and after each sad thing that I
read, you and the congregation will respond with the
words, "God is with us, even at this sad time."
(Write these words at the top of the paper.)

L: *(Read from the list)* A hurricane...

All: *(Prompt the children and congregation to respond.)*
God is with us, even at this sad time.

L: In illness...

All: God is with us, even at this sad time.

L: *(Continue down the list. Close the litany with a
prayer giving thanks for God's presence even in sad
times.)*

Delia Halverson

Christian Greetings

Scripture: Philippians 4:21

Season/Sunday: Any.

Focus: Christians greet one another in the name of Jesus.

Experience: The leader will shake the children's hands as they come forward. Toward the close of the sermon, the children will shake the hands of three people in the congregation.

Arrangements: When it's time for the children to shake hands in the congregation, if you have some very young children who are shy, you may want to quickly pair them with older kids.

> **Leader:** *(As the children come forward, shake each one's hand and say...)* "Greetings in the name of Jesus!" *(...and invite the child to be seated, until all the children have arrived).* What did I just do with my hand?
>
> **Children:** You shook our hand!
>
> **L:** Do you like to shake hands?
>
> **C:** Yes. No.
>
> **L:** Do you know why people shake hands?
>
> **C:** No!
>
> **L:** No one knows, for certain, but some people think it started as a way of showing that you don't have any weapon in your hand, that you come in peace. We do know that the earliest mention of a handshake in recorded history is in the Bible. In the book of Galatians the apostle Paul says that as he was leaving Jerusalem, where he met with James, Peter, and John, they each gave him the "right hand of fellowship." (Galatians 2:9) That's still our custom today: when we say "hello" or "good-bye" to someone, we often shake hands. And today I not only shook your hand, but I said something. What did I say?

C: You said, "Greetings in the name of Jesus!"

L: I greeted you in the name of Jesus. In one of his letters, the apostle Paul told the people to "Greet every saint in Christ Jesus." We shake hands a lot at church. This is one of the ways that we greet one another in Jesus. To practice, I'm going to ask you to go into the congregation and shake the hands of some of the people there. I want you to each shake the hands of three different people. As you do, say, "Greetings in the name of Jesus!" Ready? Go find someone, shake hands, and say,

C: *(Shaking hands with someone)* Greetings in the name of Jesus!

L: OK, that's one. Now find someone else. Ready? Shake hands...

C: Greetings in the name of Jesus!

L: That's two. Find one more person and shake hands...

C: Greetings in the name of Jesus!

L: *(When the children have finished shaking hands, call them back together.)* How did it feel to shake hands and to greet people in the name of Jesus?

C: Nice. Fun. I shook Mr. Strudwick's hand.

L: Let's say a prayer thanking God for handshakes, for Jesus, and for one another... *(prayer)*.

Barbara Younger

The Vision of God

Scripture: Joel 2:28; Acts 2

Season/Sunday: Pentecost.

Focus: To raise the question "What would the world look like if we lived with the kingdom of God as our vision?"

Experience: Children will be asked to play an imagination game and vote on several possible answers to questions.

Arrangements: You could use a selection of cards from the commercial game *Imaginiff* (Buffalo Games, Inc.), but that is not necessary as you can develop your own.

Leader:	Hi, boys and girls. Today we are going to play a game called "Imagine If." Are you ready to play?
Children:	Yes!
L:	Let's see . . . our first contestant for the day will be Pastor Geoffrey. I'll read six answers to a question. You will use your imaginations to think about the answers. Then we will raise our hands to vote on which one we think is best. Are your imaginations ready to go to work?
C:	Yes!
L:	OK, if Pastor Geoffrey were an animal which one would he be? Would he be a dog? A monkey? A koala bear? A bull? A lion? Or a frog? Are you ready to vote?
C:	Yes!
L:	OK, raise your hand if you imagine Pastor Geoffrey would be a dog; . . . how about a monkey? Oh, lots of votes there! Raise your hand if you think he would be a koala bear; . . . wow, they think you are cute and cuddly. How about a bull? A lion? And last a frog? I think the "koala bears" have it, Pastor Geoffrey!

C: *(Various responses, perhaps applause)*

L: Our next contestant is Ms. Jane, our music minister. Imagine if Ms. Jane were a circus performer: would she be a clown, a tightrope walker, a lion tamer, a juggler, a fire-eater, or a performing poodle? Are you ready to vote?

C: *(Vote for their choice as each option is repeated by leader.)*

L: Looks like you're a clown, Ms. Jane! OK, let's try one more. Imagine if all of us here loved God more than anything or anyone else. Would we all be more kind, pray every day, get everything we want, do what God wants, be more helpful, or be more loving? Use your imaginations now. What do you think? Who votes for being more kind?

C: *(Children raise hands.)*

L: Yup, I think so too. Pray every day?

C: *(Show of hands)*

L: Yes, that sounds right. Get everything we wanted *(shake head to indicate a no vote)*?

C: *(Hopefully no hands!)*

L: Nope, I agree with you; that doesn't sound right. Do what God wants *(nod head yes)*?

C: *(Raise hands.)*

L: Sure, I agree. Be more helpful?

C: *(Raise hands.)*

L: Absolutely. And how about be more loving?

C: *(Raise hands.)*

L: Yup, that's a definite. Wow! When it comes to loving God, there are lots of good answers we can all agree on. We don't have to choose just one. I love to imagine, don't you? Let's have a prayer and give thanks that our imaginations can help us live more like God wants us to . . . *(prayer)*.

Karen Evans

Let the Children Come

Scripture: Mark 10:13-16; Luke 18:15-17

Season/Sunday: Any, but Children's Sunday (on some church calendars it is the second Sunday of June) would be appropriate, or on a day when infants or children are being baptized or dedicated.

Focus: Children have a special place in the eyes of Jesus and a special place in the church.

Experience: By repeating the words of Jesus, the children will be affirmed in their worth.

Arrangements: None.

Leader: People were always coming to Jesus so that he could show his love for them, sometimes heal them, and always bless them. All kinds of people would come to Jesus, even children. Jesus loved children, and so he would say, "Let the children come to me!" Can you repeat that with me?

L & Children: "Let the children come to me!"

L: One day some parents brought their children, but the disciples tried to turn them away. But Jesus said,

Children: "Let the children come to me!"

L: Those parents were stubborn. "We want Jesus to bless them," they said. They knew that Jesus would, because Jesus said,

C: "Let the children come to me!"

L: When Jesus saw the disciples trying to turn the parents away, he was very upset. Because Jesus said,

C: "Let the children come to me!"

L: So Jesus reached out his arms and drew the children in, and they sat on his knee. Because Jesus said,

C: "Let the children come to me!"

L: Jesus laid his hands on the children and blessed them. Because Jesus said,

C: "Let the children come to me!"

L: And Jesus taught all the people saying that whoever enters the kingdom of God must become like a little child. And so Jesus taught all the people (*here indicate to the congregation that they should join in the response*) to say,

C: "Let the children come to me!"

L: That was wonderful! Let's have a prayer... *(prayer)*.

Randy Hammer

Father's Day

Scripture: Proverbs 1:8

Season/Sunday: Father's Day.

Focus: To celebrate the many things that dads teach us.

Experience: Children will act out some of the things that dads teach.

Arrangements: None.

Leader: What day is today?

Children: Father's Day! Sunday! I don't know.

L: Today is Father's Day. This is a day set aside to honor fathers! Listen to this verse from the book of Proverbs that talks about fathers: "Hear, my child, your father's instruction." God wants us to learn from our fathers. And if you don't have a father or a stepdad, you can learn from your grandpa or your uncle or other special men in your life. Let's see if we can act out some of the things that dads can teach us. *(Invite the children to stand up.)* Everyone follow my actions!

- Dads can teach us to bat *(pretend to swing a bat)*.
- And dads can teach us to swim *(pretend to swim)*.
- Dads can teach us to flip pancakes *(pretend to flip pancakes)*.
- And dads can teach us to hammer *(pretend to hammer)*.
- Dads can teach us to paint *(pretend to paint)*.
- And dads can teach us to read *(pretend to read)*.
- Dads can teach us to safely climb a ladder *(pretend to climb a ladder)*.
- And dads can teach us to pray *(fold hands and bow head)*.
- Let's all turn around and shout, "Hooray for dads!"

• *(Invite the children to share other things that dads teach us.)*

C: Hooray for dads!

L: And now let's shout "Happy Father's Day!" to all the dads.

C: Happy Father's Day!

L: Let's say a prayer thanking God for dads and the wonderful things they teach us... *(prayer)*.

Barbara Younger

Come and Seek

Scripture: Isaiah 55:1, 3, 4-7, 12

Season/Sunday: Any.

Focus: The sermon looks at the movements of worship.

Experience: The children will listen to a passage from the text and then respond with appropriate actions that demonstrate what they have heard.

Arrangements: None.

Leader: Good morning! I'd like all of the children to stand where they are, but not come forward just yet.

Children: *(Stand in place.)*

L: Today we're going to hear some verses from a book in the Bible called Isaiah. In one of the chapters in that book the prophet seems to be giving God's instructions for worship. So, whatever you hear me read from Isaiah 55, I want you to do it. Ready? "Ho, everyone who thirsts, / **come** to the waters;" *(indicate with your hand for children to come forward as you continue to read)* "and you that have no money, / **come**, buy and eat! / **Come**, buy wine and milk / without money and without price" (Isaiah 55:1).

C: *(Come forward.)*

L: That was great! OK, so we all came when God called us. Let's *listen* to what God says next: "**Incline** your ear, and come to me; *(tilt your head and cup your ear, indicating children should do the same)* / **listen**, so that you may live. / I will make with you an everlasting covenant, / my steadfast, sure love for David" (Isaiah 55:3). So, what does Isaiah tell us to do after we come?

C: To listen!

58

L: That's right. And what is it we hear when we listen to God?

C: *(Various replies)*

L: Good answers! We hear about how God loves us and how God wants us to live. Now here's the next part: "**See**," *(put hand as shade for eyes, as if scanning the horizon)* "I made him a witness to the peoples, / a leader and commander for the peoples. / **See**, you shall call nations that you do not know, /and nations that do not know you shall run to you, / because of the LORD your God, the Holy One of Israel, / for he has glorified you" (Isaiah 55:4-5). So after we come and listen the next thing we do is to . . . ?

C: See!

L: And what do we see when we look around at all that God has done?

C: *(Various replies)*

L: Those are good answers too—we see how much God loves us just in all of the beautiful things God has given us. Ready for the next part?

C: Yes!

L: "**Seek** the LORD while he may be found." How could we seek the Lord?

C: *(May or may not have any ideas.)*

L: Well, let's keep listening to what Isaiah has to say, "**Seek** the LORD while he may be found, / **call** upon him while he is near; let the wicked forsake their way, and the unrighteous their thoughts; / let them return to the LORD, that he may have mercy on them, / and to our God, for he will abundantly pardon" (Isaiah 55:6-7). So, at least in these verses, to "seek the Lord" seems to have to do with repentance, with saying we're sorry for our sins; then God pardons us. Maybe we could bow down as a motion to show we're sorry *(leader and children bow)*, and then God "abundantly" pardons us *(stand up slowly, showing relief)*, and we all feel so much better! Do you feel better knowing God has pardoned you?

C: Yes!

L: OK, in the last part of the chapter God says through Isaiah, "For you shall **go out** in joy, / and be led back in peace; / the mountains and the hills before you / shall burst into song, / and all the trees of the field shall clap their hands" (Isaiah 55:12). It says that we are to "go out" and that we will do so with so much joy that even the mountains will sing and the trees will clap their hands. Have you ever heard a tree clap its hands?

C: No!

L: Are you sure? *(Start to sway like a tree in the wind.)* What happens when the wind blows, and a tree starts to sway back and forth, and then its leaves rustle together? It's a lot like clapping! Let's have a prayer and give thanks to the Lord for the way we are invited to come and listen and seek and see, and then to go out with joy... *(prayer).*

And now, as we leave, let's ask the congregation to flutter their hands together to provide some clapping leaf sounds as we go and tell others all that God has done for us...

Congregation: *(Provide sound as requested.)*

Brant D. Baker

Symbols

Scripture: Deuteronomy 6:4-9

Season/Sunday: Any.

Focus: To introduce some of the symbols of Christianity to the children.

Experience: The children will explore the symbols that you have in your place of worship (and/or elsewhere in your church buildings) and relate them to symbols they are familiar with in the community.

Arrangements: Make drawings of symbols around your community (or if preferred, download from the Internet); use symbols for such things as restrooms; handicapped parking, traffic signs, no smoking, school crossing, and others. Explore your place of worship for symbols that convey our Christian faith. You may also bring in symbols or pictures of symbols that are used elsewhere in the buildings. Choose the explanations below that are appropriate to your congregation.

     Leader: Good morning! I have some drawings that may be familiar to you. What do these mean? (*Hold up one symbol after another for them to identify.*)

    Children: (Varied responses)

        L: These are symbols that we see around our community. They are like talking with pictures. We have symbols that we use in our church too. Some of them are here in this room, and some are elsewhere in our buildings. Let's look at some of the symbols. (*Ask the children to move with you to the place where some of the symbols are displayed in your worship area. The ones that were brought in or the pictures you took of symbols can be explained as you sit together. Be sure to use symbols that you find in the architecture, such as circles, squares, triangles,* *and arches, as well as those that are obvious.*)

- Arch: God is over us as the heavens above
- Bread/wheat and chalice/grapes: Communion
- Candle: Christ is the light of the world
- Circle: God's eternal love
- Colors (seasonal):
  Purple (Advent = royalty, getting ready for the King; Lent = penitence, admitting our mistakes)
  Blue (Advent = hope)
  White (Christmas and Communion = purity)
  Green (Epiphany and Ordinary Seasons = growth, outreach)
  Red (Pentecost = flame of Holy Spirit)
- Cross: Christ died for us and has power over death
- Dove: Peace or Holy Spirit
- Flame: Holy Spirit
- Rainbow: God's covenant with us
- Square (or anything with four parts): Four Gospels (Matthew, Mark, Luke, John)
- Stained glass window: The story/message the picture tells
- Triangle (or anything with 3 parts): Trinity (Father, Son, Holy Spirit)
- Water or baptismal font: Washed clean at baptism

L: These are some of the symbols that help us understand more about God and about what we believe. Let's have a prayer and thank God for the symbols of our faith . . . (*prayer*).

Delia Halverson

Fourth of July

Scripture: Psalm 85:12

Season/Sunday: Fourth of July or another national holiday.

Focus: To think about the beauty of our country and give thanks to God for it.

Experience: The children will go into the congregation to learn what five or more people think is most beautiful about America. At the close of the sermon, the children will hear and/or sing the song "America the Beautiful."

Arrangements: If you don't have five children who are old enough to go into the congregation and return with a response, recruit older kids to help you. If this isn't practical, you can invite the congregation to call out responses to the question: "What do you think is most beautiful about America?" Plan on having your choir or entire congregation sing the song "America the Beautiful" at the close of the sermon. The song is included in most hymnals and is in the public domain, so you are free to take it from another source if need be. If this isn't practical, perhaps you can find a CD or tape with the song, or have a soloist sing the first verse.

Leader:	What country do we celebrate on the Fourth of July?
Children:	America. The United States. Our country.
L:	The Fourth of July is a holiday set aside to celebrate our country, the United States of America. And there's lots to celebrate! We live in a country that is beautiful in many ways. I'd like five volunteers to go out into the congregation and ask five people what they think is most beautiful about America and then come back and tell us what they heard *(choose five children)*.
	(Continue while they are gone) In the Psalms there is a verse that says "The Lord will give what is

good, / and our land will yield its increase." Of course this isn't about America, but it is safe to say that God does desire to give all countries good things and has made nature to give lots of good things when it is cared for.

(When the children return, ask them to tell you what they heard. Repeat their responses so everyone can hear. You may want to add some additional responses such as your favorite vacation place, an important historical site, a beloved American food or pastime, and so on.)

There are many beautiful things about America. In 1893, a young woman named Katharine Lee Bates took a trip to the top of Pikes Peak. As she looked from the top of this high mountain, words about the beauty of America came into her mind. She wrote them in a poem that became a famous song. Let's sing that song right now! *(Have everyone sing the song.)* That's a beautiful song about our beautiful country. Our country has been blessed in many ways as the song tells us. Let's say a prayer thanking God for our country and its beauty... *(prayer).*

Barbara Younger

The God Who Delivers

Scripture: The Book of Jonah; specifically, Jonah 2:9

Season/Sunday: Any.

Focus: God as a delivering God who loves all people and all creation.

Experience: The children will learn to embrace the idea of God as a loving, delivering God through the story and responses.

Arrangements: None.

Leader: Good morning! Today we are going to talk about a prophet. Can anyone tell us what a prophet is? (*Give a moment for responses, affirming answers when possible.*) Long before the time of Jesus, a prophet was someone who spoke God's message to the world. One such prophet was Jonah, and this morning we're going to tell his story together. Let's stand up, and when I do a motion, you do the same, and when I give you a response, you repeat it when the time is right. Are you ready? Let's go!

God called Jonah (*place your hands by your mouth as though calling out and wait for children to mimic*) wanting him to go to the city of Nineveh to preach this message: "Deliverance comes from the Lord!" Can you repeat that with me?

All: Deliverance comes from the Lord!

L: But Jonah refused and ran (*run in place*), and caught a ship going the other way. A storm came up on the sea, and the waves rolled (*make a rolling motion with your arm*) and rolled. Everyone on the ship was worried, but they really didn't need to be because,

All: Deliverance comes from the Lord!

L: The sailors rowed (*make rowing motion with your arms*) and rowed, but could not keep the ship afloat.

They got even more worried but...

All: Deliverance comes from the Lord!

L: Finally Jonah admitted that the whole mess was his fault and that the best thing to do was for them to throw him into the sea. A great fish swallowed (*motion with your hand as a fish swallowing*) him whole. Now do you suppose Jonah was worried? Maybe he was, but if anyone knew, Jonah knew that...

All: Deliverance comes from the Lord!

L: Jonah prayed (*fold hands as though praying*), and the fish spat him out because...

All: Deliverance comes from the Lord!

L: Again God called to Jonah (*place your hands by your mouth as though calling out*), asking him to preach and give the people of Nineveh the message...

All: Deliverance comes from the Lord!

L: This time Jonah obeyed and preached (*raise your arms in the air as though exhorting*) to the people of Nineveh saying...

All: Deliverance comes from the Lord!

L: They believed and turned to God. And God said, "I love (*place your hand over your heart*) all people, and I love all animals, too." And all the people praised God because...

All: Deliverance comes from the Lord!

L: That was excellent—thanks for helping me tell the story. Let's have a prayer and give thanks for God's deliverance... (*prayer*).

Randy Hammer

The Invitation

Scripture: Matthew 22:1-10

Season/Sunday: Any, or a Communion Sunday.

Focus: God's great invitation to all people.

Experience: Children will observe various reactions to Jesus' invitation, and then help invite others.

Arrangements: Arrange for four helpers. The first comes and laughs at the invitation, the second refuses because he or she is too busy, the third and fourth together get angry and storm off.

Leader:	How many of you have ever been to a party?
Children:	I have! It was my birthday party.
L:	Jesus told a story once about a king who threw a big party. It was in celebration of his son's marriage. They had all kinds of good stuff to eat, the best food anywhere in all the town. And the king sent out invitations (*motion for first helper to come forward*).
L:	(*Say excitedly to the helper*) You have been invited to the king's feast. His son is getting married!
Helper 1:	(*Walks away, laughing uncontrollably*) What a silly idea that is. Who would want to go to a wedding party? Ha! Ha! Ha!
L:	Well fortunately, the king had invited some more people (*motion for helper number two to come forward.*) You have been invited to the king's party. It's a wedding party for his son. He is getting married.
Helper 2:	(*Looks irritated*) I don't have time for a party! I'm too busy. I've got to go; leave me alone.
L:	Well, fortunately, the king had invited some other people (*motion for the remaining two helpers to come forward*). Guess what, you have been especially invited to the king's party. He is throwing a big celebration for his son who is getting married.

Helpers 3&4: (*Looking angry*) How dare you invite us to a party! Who do you think you are? We don't want to go to any old king's party! *(Storm away.)*

L: No one the king invited wanted to attend. Some thought it was silly, some were too busy, and some just didn't like the invitation and no one quite knows why. So you know what the king did next?

C: What?

L: He sent his messengers out into the streets and invited anyone who would come. I'm going to need some help here—will you be the messengers and go out into the congregation and invite anyone who will to come to the Communion Table?

C: (*Children go out into the congregation and give invitations; children and invitees gather around the table.*)

L: One of the meals we eat together in God's name is called the Lord's Supper. When we eat the Lord's Supper, we can remember we are all invited to God's great banquet. Let's have a prayer and thank God that everyone is invited . . . (*prayer*).

Jeff Hutcheson

Parting the Red Sea

Scripture: Exodus 14:21-31

Season/Sunday: Any.

Focus: There is a lot to be afraid of in this world, for children and adults alike. Whether we are being chased by Pharaoh's army or facing the fears of modern life, God calls us to trust.

Experience: To be present at the parting of the Red Sea by having the children become the children of Israel, having the ushers become Pharaoh's army, and having the congregation become the waters of the Red Sea.

Arrangements: Have at least four ushers or other adults on hand who know their cue and are ready to give chase to the "children of Israel." A printed word of instruction in the bulletin might help the congregation get into the action more quickly.

Leader: Would the children meet me at the back of the church, please? Today we're going to pretend that we're the children of Israel, the Hebrew nation, escaping from the Egyptians. Do you remember that story? How Moses led the people out into the wilderness to escape from Pharaoh; how they came up against the Red Sea and couldn't cross with Pharaoh's armies closing in behind them. Well, we're going to do all that, so first of all we need somebody to be Moses *(choose a child)*. Good, you're Moses, and you come down here to the front of the children of Israel.

Congregation, we need your help. We need everybody to stand up and move into the aisle to become the Red Sea. Pretend that you're the ocean, if you want to do the Wave, that's fine.

OK, here's what happened. *(Read Exodus 14:21)* "Then Moses stretched out his hand over the sea ..."

69

OK, Moses stretch out your hand...very good!
"The LORD drove the sea back by a strong east wind all night, and turned the sea into dry land; and the waters were divided." *(Congregation should move back into pews, but make sure they don't sit down.)*

Great! Now the children of Israel went on through....Congregation, don't sit down!...Moses, lead your nation on through here, all the children of Israel walking through on dry land.

(After arriving at the front of the church)
Where's Moses? Moses, it says here that when all of the people got through, they looked back, and what did they see but the Egyptians! *(Cue for ushers)*
Look at those menacing Egyptians! And it says that Moses raised his hand,...Hurry Moses, raise your hand...and the ocean came back together.
(Congregation should catch their cue) Whew! Well what does all this mean, why is it important? Moses, what does this tell us?

Child: I don't know.

L: Anybody have any ideas?

Children: God will protect us? God will drown the Egyptians? To pray to God?

L: To pray to God, I think you're right. Because God is interested in us and wants to help us and is active in our lives, so we don't need to be afraid when we feel like there's no escape from our problems. Like Moses we can lift our hands in prayer and ask God to take over. Well, let's all lift our hands right now and ask God's help and thank God for the way we're taken care of...*(prayer)*.

Brant D. Baker

How to Play? The Ten Commandments

Scripture: Exodus 19:16–20:17

Season/Sunday: Any.

Focus: This sermon focuses on the Ten Commandments, the guidance given to the Israelites about how to live together in community. After they left Egypt and were wandering in the strange lands, the Israelites needed guidance in how to live together as a community.

Experience: The children will attempt to play a game without knowing the rules to the game. This experience will be related to the experience of the Israelites wandering in the wilderness. The children will hear a paraphrase of the Ten Commandments. Note that the objective of this sermon is to understand *not* the content of the Ten Commandments but the purpose of having the Ten Commandments.

Arrangements: You will need a deck of cards or a partial deck of cards (perhaps leave out the face cards) to help the game go faster. Have the children sit in a circle, so that each person can see the center of the circle. You'll be using the center to play a game with the cards.

Leader:	Good morning everyone! Today is going to be so much fun. This morning, we are going to play a card game. Do you want to play?
Children:	Yeah!
L:	Wonderful! OK, I have a deck of cards here, and each of you will receive one card *(Distribute cards—if you have enough, you can give two to each child. Note: If you have a large group of children, you may want to ask who wants to play and select a small group of children to play, or ask an adult helper to form a second group)*. OK, ready to play?
C:	Yeah!

L: All right, let's play. *(Place card in the middle. Then look at the children and wait for a few seconds.)* Um...I said, let's play. Who's next?

C: *(The children look confused.)*

L: Come on, let's get the game going!

C: But we don't know how to play. How do we play the game?

L: Oh goodness, did I forget to give you the rules to the game?

C: Yes!

L: I guess you can't play the game if you don't know the rules. All right, here's how we play. You can put a card down if you have the same number or the same suit. Suit is the shape *(show them)*: a heart, a spade, a club, or a diamond that you see on the card. If you can't put down the card, you say, "Pass." The game is over when everyone has no more cards or everyone passes. Now, let's play *(play the game)*. Thank you for playing the game. It was a lot more fun once we all knew the rules, wasn't it?

C: Yes!

L: Let me tell you a story of a group of people who also didn't know the rules and were confused. Some of you may remember the story of Moses and how he helped a group of people called the Israelites escape from Egypt. When the Israelites left Egypt to live in the strange lands, they didn't know how to live together. They were confused just like we were confused when we tried to play the game without knowing the rules. God saw this and decided to give them rules to help them live peacefully. Do you know what these rules are?

C: Use your indoor voices?

L: Well, something like that. God gave the people ten rules to live by, only ten, so that they could count them on two hands. And do you know what we call those ten rules?

C: The Ten Commandments!

L: Good, let's learn them together and count them with our hands *(have the children hold up a finger with you for each commandment, and echo what you say).* Number 1 *(hold up a finger, and throughout, for each commandment)*: Have no other god but God.

C: *(Echo.)*

L: Number 2: Worship only God.

C: *(Echo.)*

L: Number 3: Honor God's name.

C: *(Echo.)*

L: Number 4: Remember and keep God's sabbath holy.

C: *(Echo.)*

L: Number 5: Honor your parents.

C: *(Echo.)*

L: Number 6: Do not murder.

C: *(Echo.)*

L: Number 7: Keep your marriage promises.

C: *(Echo.)*

L: Number 8: Do not steal.

C: *(Echo.)*

L: Number 9: Do not lie.

C: *(Echo.)*

L: Number 10: Do not be envious of others.

C: *(Echo.)*

L: *(Keeping ten fingers up)* These are our Ten Commandments. Let's bring our commandments together *(clasp fingers of both hands together)*, hold them to our hearts *(bring clasped hands to the heart)*, and give thanks for God's guidance, God's rules that help us know how to live . . . *(prayer)*.

Joyce S. Fong

Serve the Lord with Gladness!

Scripture: Psalm 100

Season/Sunday: Any.

Focus: This sermon focuses on giving one's entire being to God in worship.

Experience: The children and the congregation will be invited to give thanks and enact motions to various prompts in Psalm 100.

Arrangements: Besides a Bible or copy of Psalm 100 the leader only needs plenty of energy to put some grand fun into worship!

> **Leader:** Good morning everyone! Today we are going to praise God with our whole body, but first I want to ask you a question: does anyone know what a psalm is?
>
> **Children:** The Bible? Psalms are words?
>
> **L:** That's partly right: a Psalm is simply a *song*. In ancient times people sang the psalms because they were songs that they used in worship. So part of what we are going to do today is sing. OK. Everybody ready? Let's stand up so that we can do what the psalm says, and, Congregation, why don't you help us too? Everybody on your feet! OK, repeat after me: "Make a joyful noise to the LORD, all the earth!"
>
> **All:** *(Echo.)*
>
> **L:** "Worship the LORD with gladness!"
>
> **All:** *(Echo.)*
>
> **L:** "Come into his presence with singing."
>
> **All:** *(Echo.)*
>
> **L:** OK, let's sing to the Lord! And clap! "Hallalu, Hallelu, Hallelu, Hallelujah: Praise ye the Lord!" Congregation, help us clap and sing...
>
> **All:** *(Echo.)*

L: Good! Now here's what's next, repeat it after me: "Know that the LORD is God."

All: *(Echo.)*

L: "It is he that made us, and we are his"

All: *(Echo.)*

L: "We are his people, and the sheep of his pasture."

All: *(Echo.)*

L: So if we are God's sheep and God made us and loves us, let's pretend that God is giving us a hug right now *(wrap arms around your own shoulders in demonstration)* and say "Thank you, Lord." Congregation, you too!

All: Thank you, Lord.

L: That was great! Here's what's next, "Enter [God's] gates with thanksgiving, /and his courts with praise."

All: *(Echo.)*

L: "Give thanks to [God], bless his name."

All: *(Echo.)*

L: So to give thanks and bless God's name, let's fold our hands like we are praying and say, "Thank you, Lord!"

All: *(Hands folded)* Thank you, Lord!

L: Good! OK, last part, "For the LORD is good"

All: *(Echo.)*

L: "His steadfast love . . . and faithfulness endure forever."

All: *(Echo.)*

L: So the Lord is good and faithful to us. Since that's true, let's lift our hands high into the air toward God in praise and say "Thank you, Lord!"

All: *(Reaching upward)* Thank you, Lord!

L: Thank you, Lord, indeed! Amen! *(Option: repeat as closing prayer, or offer separate prayer.)*

Bob Sharman

Looking for Ways to Help

Scripture: Luke 16:19-31

Season/Sunday: Any.

Focus: If we will pay attention, we will see people who need our help every day.

Experience: The children will view pictures of persons who might be in need of some help and give some ideas about how they could help.

Arrangements: Gather pictures from magazines, newspapers, books, or online that show people in various situations, such as a person crying, a homeless person, a child with a disability, a child who is hungry, a child who is left out of games with others or who has broken a toy.

Leader:	Good morning, I'm really glad to see you here today! Have you ever heard the story Jesus told about two men, one who was very rich and one who was very poor?
Children:	*(Various replies)*
L:	The rich man had everything he needed, but he only thought about himself. The poor man was not only poor but also hungry and sick, and he spent his days lying outside the rich man's gate. But the rich man did nothing to help the poor man; it was like he didn't even notice him. I hope we're not like that, but sometimes see people who need our help. I thought we could spend some time thinking of ways we could help people in need. For example, here's a picture of a woman who is crying. What might we do to help her?
C:	You could give her a tissue. You could tell her it is going to get better. You could ask why is she crying.
L:	Those are all excellent ideas! What about this one?

This family has lost its home during a hurricane, and they have nowhere to live and only the things in this cart. What could we do?

C: We could send some supplies for school. Raise money for a new home. We could give them some food.

L: Those are more great ideas! How about this one? These children are in wheelchairs. What might they need?

C: You could help them with the money for an operation so maybe they could walk. You could carry their stuff around school and help push them. You could be friends with them and ask them to your house.

L: You are all so good at this! What about this one? This child seems to be sad because she broke her crayon.

C: That one is easy—you just give her some of yours. That's all there is to that one.

L: Well, OK, you've got that solved! Every day, if we pay attention and keep our eyes open, we will see people who need our help. Today when you leave here and every day this week, let's all be on the lookout for people we can help. You've given us some great ideas. Now let's ask God to help us go out and do it... *(prayer)*.

Karen Evans

God's Love Is Forever

Scripture: Psalm 136:1

Season/Sunday: Any.

Focus: God's love is forever.

Experience: The children will catch bubbles and try to save them.

Arrangements: You will need a bottle of bubbles. Consider purchasing bubbles to send home with the children, with a kind warning not to open them in church.

Leader: *(Hold up the bottle of bubbles.)* Here's something fun! What are these?

Children: Bubbles!

L: I know you are all very clever and very good at catching things. I'm going to blow bubbles. I want each of you to catch one. *(Blow lots of bubbles.)*

C: I got one! Here's one! I have two!

L: Good work! Now I'm going to blow bubbles again. This time I want you each to catch a bubble and save it. *(Blow more bubbles. Pause for a few seconds after you stop blowing bubbles.)* Now show me your bubbles. *(If children still have bubbles left, admire them. Wait a few more seconds until all the bubbles pop.)* Does anyone have a bubble left?

C: No!

L: Bubbles are beautiful, but they only last for a moment or two. There's only one thing that lasts forever. The Bible says to give thanks to the Lord, "for God's steadfast love will last forever." Let's say together, "God's love lasts forever."

All: God's love lasts forever!

L: We can just have a bubble for a little while, but...

All: God's love lasts forever!

L: Flowers fade and tadpoles turn into frogs, but...

All: God's love lasts forever!
  L: Toys get broken and sometimes even the things we
         love the most on this earth get taken from us, but...
All: God's love lasts forever!
  L: Let's say a prayer celebrating God and God's forever
         love... *(prayer)*.

Barbara Younger

Helpers of God

Scripture: Deuteronomy 2:7

Season/Sunday: Labor Day or Any.

Focus: To expand the focus of God's helpers beyond the church and into the community.

Experience: The children will examine different hats or other objects that symbolize various community helpers and explore ways that these persons are also helpers of God. The children will also connect their findings with members of the congregation.

Arrangements: Collect various hats or other objects from workers in the community, such as firefighter, construction worker, police, teacher, bus driver, chef, doctor, or nurse.

> **Leader:** Good morning! What do these hats and other things here remind you of?
>
> **Children:** *(Varied responses)*
>
> **L:** You are right! All of these represent someone who helps us in our community. *(Take time to allow the children to try on some of the hats or handle the objects and tell what helper each represents.)*
>
> **C:** *(Varied responses)*
>
> **L:** You know, these are not only community helpers, but they are also God's helpers. Sometimes we think that God's helpers are only the people who work in the church, but we can all be God's helpers when we do things that are helpful to other people. What are some ways that you can be God's helper?
>
> **C:** *(Varied responses)*
>
> **L:** Let's thank God for the many helpers in our community and ask God to show us ways that we can be helpers every day... *(prayer)*.

Delia Halverson

Honoring Teachers

Scripture: 1 Thessalonians 5:12-13

Season/Sunday: Any, but most appropriate for a day set aside to commission or dedicate teachers for the coming year.

Focus: To esteem in love those who serve through teaching.

Experience: The children will bring teachers forward and will lay hands on them for a blessing.

Arrangements: None are needed, although an optional ending for this sermon would be to have them repeat a liturgical blessing after the leader. This blessing could either be something the leader writes or something out of your church's liturgical tradition.

  Leader: Good morning. Who can tell me what happens next Monday?

  Children: School starts!

  L: That's right! And did you know that today our own new year of Sunday school starts too? So today we're going to pray for all of the teachers—the Sunday school teachers, the elementary school teachers, the junior and senior high school teachers, even the college professors. The Bible says that we are "to respect those who labor among you, and have charge of you in the Lord and admonish you; [and that we should] esteem them very highly in love because of their work." So, here's what we're going to do: I'm going to ask all of the teachers in the congregation to stand *(indicate that they should do so)* and I'm going to ask all of you *(pointing to children)* to go and take a teacher by the hand and bring them up here.

  C: *(Disperse to collect teachers; children may need to* *make more than one trip depending on numbers.)*

L: *(Once all have been gathered)* OK, now, in the Bible there is a special way of praying for people and blessing them. It's called "laying on of hands" and means we simply and gently put our hands on the person or people we are praying for. Will you join me now in laying your hands on these teachers *(option: teachers could be invited to kneel, as they are able).*

C: *(Lay on hands.)*

L: Let's pray... *(prayer, or "repeat after me this blessing...").*

Brant D. Baker

Follow Me!

Scripture: Mark 1:16-20

Season/Sunday: Any.

Focus: Jesus calls us to follow him. We can invite others to join us to follow Jesus, too.

Experience: The children will have the opportunity to fish for followers of Jesus and invite them to come forward to hear about Jesus.

Arrangements: Have several toy or homemade fishing poles that the children will use to "fish" for people to join them up front to hear about Jesus this week. Prior to the sermon speak with one or two children to let them know that you will start the fishing process with them. (**Explain how they will "fish" with the poles without hurting the other children.**) Consider the number of children that you usually have for the sermon time. If it's a large number, get two or three children to go fishing for each other at the same time.

Leader:	Good morning, everyone! Today, I thought we'd do something a little different to get us all up front. I've got a fishing pole here, and since Jesus tells his followers that he will make them fish for people, that's what we're going to do—fish for people! After I catch a people fish, I'll let that person help in catching other people fish. So, here I go . . . oh, boy, looks like I caught a big fish today! Hey, Jennie, now it is your turn. Who are you going to fish for?
Jennie:	My best friend, Sari! (*Jennie goes to fish for Sari, and then passes the pole on to her, while leader continues fishing for other children.*)
L:	Looks like Jennie caught Sari! Who are you going to fish for?

Sari: Miguel!

L: Make sure we catch all those people fish! Don't leave anyone out! *(Once all the children have gathered up front)* In the Bible story we heard (*or, Jesus tells a Bible story in which . . .*), Jesus calls his disciples as they were fishing for fish. He tells them that he will make them fish for people. How can we fish for people? What are some of the things that we can do to invite them to be followers of Jesus?

Children: We can use a fishing pole. We can invite them to church. We can bring them to Sunday school. We can tell them about Jesus.

L: That's right. We can do all those things. Think about how you might be a fisher of people and who you might invite to come hear about Jesus. Remember that Jesus wants us to follow him and fish for people. So what are we going to do?

C: Follow him! Fish for people!

L: Now let's thank God for calling us to be followers of Jesus and ask God to make us good fishers of people . . . *(prayer).*

Susan M. Lang

Following God's Path

Scripture: Psalm 25:4

Season/Sunday: Any.

Focus: The Bible helps us know how God wants us to live.

Experience: A child and an older helper will lay out a yarn path along the aisle of the church. After this is done, the leader will take the children down the path.

Arrangements: Most churches have an aisle long enough to lay out a simple yarn path. If this isn't practical, perhaps a smaller path can be laid out in the front of the church. Use thick yarn since thinner yarn may be difficult for the child to unroll. Recruit a teen or adult helper. Have a Bible handy from which to read the verse.

Leader: *(Holding up the ball of yarn)* This may look like an ordinary ball of yarn, but today we're going to do something very important with it. We're going to lay out a path. I need a volunteer to lay out a path down the aisle of the church.

Children: I will! I will!

L: I'm going to let *(child's name)* help us today along with *(helper.)* You can make a straight path or a squiggly one down the aisle. *(The helper can hold one end of the yarn as the child unrolls it.)* While we wait for our yarn path, I want you to tell me about any paths or trails you have walked.

C: I walk on the sidewalk near my house. There is a nature path at my school. My grandma has a path to her pond.

L: Those all sound like wonderful paths! It looks like our yarn path is finished. Let's all follow it! *(Lead the children on the path. As you do, say things like "This is a great path," "The path helps me know* *how to go," "Thanks, (child's name and helper) for making this path." When you get to the end of the path, turn everyone around and walk the path back up to the front. Invite the children to sit down again.)* There is a verse in the Bible that talks about paths *(open Bible and read Psalm 25:4).* The person who wrote these words was asking God to show the path of how we should live. *(Close the Bible and hold it up.)* The Bible is like a path. The words in the Bible tell us how God wants us to live. If we follow the path of the Bible, then we are following God's path. Let's all say together, "The Bible is God's path!"

C: The Bible is God's path!

L: When we don't know which way to go, we can find out because,

C: The Bible is God's path!

L: If we're lost in life, we don't need to worry because,

C: The Bible is God's path!

L: Let's have a prayer thanking God for the Bible . . . *(prayer). (After sermon have helper roll up the yarn.)*

Barbara Younger

A Person of Peace

Scripture: Matthew 10:5-14

Season/Sunday: Any, but could be good for Missions or Evangelism Sunday.

Focus: The sermon looks at Jesus' mission instructions, to find a person of peace with whom to share the gospel as part of the initial invitation to a new group of people or different culture.

Experience: The children will announce the good news twice, once to a person who does not receive it, a second time to someone who does.

Arrangements: The leader will need two helpers who will position themselves behind two separate closed doors in the worship space, preferably without being seen. Each helper will need to know his or her brief dialogue as shown below.

> **Leader:** Good morning! In the scripture we just heard, Jesus gives his followers *(or, Jesus tells his disciples)* instructions on how to take the Good News to a new place. He says that we should travel with few possessions, and that we are to do good deeds as we go and proclaim the good news that the kingdom of God has come near. Jesus also tells his followers that when they go into a new village, they should find someone who will receive a greeting of peace, someone Jesus calls a "person of peace." Hey, I have an idea, let's go see if we can find a person of peace around here. Will you come with me?
>
> **Children:** Yes!
>
> **L:** *(Lead children on brief journey to first closed door, explaining as you go . . .)* All right, when we get to the door let's all say "Peace be to this house." Can you practice that with me? Ready,
>
> **C:** Peace be to this house.

L: That was good. And if they welcome us we'll share with them the good news that the kingdom of God has come near. OK, here we are *(knock on door).*

Helper 1: *(Opens door just enough to be heard, person doesn't need to be seen)* Hello?

C: Peace be to this house.

Helper 1: Go away, don't bother me!

L: Oh, OK, sorry to disturb you *(turn to leave, heading toward second door).* You know, as part of his instructions Jesus says to shake the dust off your shoes when that happens. Why do you suppose he says that?

C: *(Various answers)*

L: Those are good guesses *(or, "That's right ...")*, in Bible times shaking off dust from one's feet was a way of saying your responsibility had ended *(Oxford New Revised Standard Version,* note on Acts 13:51). OK, well, here we are at someone else's door. Remember to say "Peace be to this house" when someone answers, OK? Here we go *(knock on door).*

Helper 2: *(Cracking door)* Hello?

C: Peace be to this house.

Helper 2: *(Opening door completely)* And also with you.

Child: That's my daddy *(This has actually happened, and the little guy was surprised!)*

L: *(To helper 2)* We have good news to share with you, the kingdom of God has come near! *(To the children)* Let's have a prayer and thank God for the good news we have to share ... *(prayer).*

Brant D. Baker

Invited to the Table of God

Scripture: Luke 14:15-23

Season/Sunday: World Communion Sunday.

Focus: God's home is open to everyone. God invites all of us to share a meal together in his kingdom. Our only responsibility is to attend!

Experience: Everyone is invited to the Table of God to take communion. Some adults in the pew pretend to leave the service because they need to attend other important events. The children remain and (if this is part of your faith tradition) are invited to partake in the Lord's Supper.

Arrangements: Usual Holy Communion setup. Preselect several adults to interrupt the children's sermon.

> **Leader:** (*Without calling the children forward*) Blessed is anyone who will eat bread in the kingdom of God. Once again, we come to this table of God because God invited us to celebrate and remem...
>
> **Interrupter 1:** (*Gets up*) Oh, I'm so sorry. Thanks for the invitation, but I can't stay. I just bought a new house and I need to go see it.
>
> **L:** (*Looking bothered*) Ahem...as I was saying, once again, we come to this table of...
>
> **Interrupter 2:** (*Gets up*) Oh, I'm sorry too. I have to go. I just bought a new DVD player, and I want to test it out.
>
> **L:** (*Looking even more bothered*) We come to this table of God because God invited us to celebrate and remem...
>
> **Interrupter 3:** (*Gets up*) My apologies, but my best friend is getting married. I need to go now to get to his wedding.
>
> **L:** Children, would you please come up and gather around the table of God?

Children: (*Children hesitantly approach the area.*)

  L: Wow, thank you all for coming when I invited you. Jesus once told a story about someone who planned a great dinner and invited many people. When the dinner was ready, he asked all those who were invited to come. But just like today, many who were invited began making excuses and didn't come. So the host invited other people who were not usually invited to these parties like the poor, the sick, the crippled, the blind, and the lame. Jesus told this story to show that God invites everyone, children too, to come to the feast in God's kingdom. Sharing the Lord's Supper can help us remember God's invitation to the great feast in heaven.

Interrupters: Hey, we changed our minds. We want to come to the Lord's Supper, too!

  L: That's great! Welcome back! Let's all pray and prepare our hearts for the Lord's Supper... (*prayer*).

Joyce S. Fong

The Parable of the Laborers in the Vineyard

Scripture: Matthew 20:1-16

Season/Sunday: Any.

Focus: God's grace is a generous gift.

Experience: The children will become the workers as they experience the parable of the vineyard.

Arrangements: Determine a section of the congregation to be the vineyard. If the choir is accessible, they will make an excellent vineyard; if not, a small section of the congregation will suffice. If the choir, supply in advance with bundles of artificial grapes (or have some ready to distribute), a piggy bank full of dimes, and a bowl. Be sure the piggy bank is of the type that you can get into easily to distribute the money when needed.

Leader: Good morning! Today we're going to hear the story Jesus told about a vineyard and some workers. Have you ever heard it?

Children: *(Various responses)*

L: *(Produce piggy bank)* Once upon a time there was a wealthy landowner *(shake bank)*, I mean really wealthy! *(Open the bank and pour out some of the money.)*

C: *(Giggles)* I have a bank like that!

L: This landowner had a vineyard *(ask the choir or the group you have selected to stand and hold out their arms like vines)*. In this vineyard grew lots of grapes *(choir produces grapes or distribute)*. One year this vineyard produced lots and lots of grapes; it was the best year the landowner ever had. There were so many grapes the owner decided to hire more help to pick them all. So he went out early in the morning, about six o'clock, to hire more help. *(Addressing two children)* "Would you like to work in my vineyard? I'll pay you a day's wage."

2 Children: Yes!

  L: *(Ask them to go to the vineyard and pretend to pick grapes.)* The owner realized that more help was needed, so he went back out to the town about nine o'clock that morning to look for more help *(ask two more child volunteers in the same manner as before. Only this time say "I'll pay you what's right." Repeat this same process for twelve noon; three o'clock; and finally five o'clock).*

    At the end of the day the owner called for his manager *(select another volunteer and lead him or her to stand next to the bowl, which the leader should now fill with dimes from the piggy bank).* The owner instructed his manager to pay each worker their wages starting with the last and finishing with the first *(instruct all the workers to line up, from those who worked last in the day to those who worked first).*

    One by one the workers came to receive their pay. Those who had worked last, for only one hour, received a dime *(the manager hands them their dime, and they go sit down).* At this point the people in the back of the line, the ones who worked the whole day, got excited. They figured that if the ones who worked only an hour were getting a day's pay, a whole dime, then they were going to get much, much more.

  C: *(Act excited.)*

  L: Those who came to work at three o'clock received a dime *(manager hands them each their pay, repeat this process for each, emphasizing how much they get paid).* Now the workers near the end of the line were starting to get worried, and even began to grumble a little bit.

  C: *(Start to grumble.)*

  L: Finally those who came at six o'clock who had been in the hot sun and worked all day long received *(manager hands them their pay)* . . . a dime. What did you think of that story?

  C: It's not fair.

L: Why not?

C: Because they worked all day and should have gotten more pay.

L: That's what I thought too. And some of the workers complained about that very thing. You know what the manager said?

C: No.

L: It's my money; I can pay people what I want to. Didn't you receive what you agreed to get? Are you upset because I am so generous? (*pause*) Jesus said we can learn something about God from this parable. That God is like the landowner: very, very generous. So generous in fact that God will offer the same love and salvation even to those of us who show up late. Let's have a prayer and give thanks that our God is so generous... (*prayer*).

Jeff Hutcheson

Gospel Changes

Scripture: Matthew 21:12-13

Season/Sunday: Any.

Focus: We read in the Gospels that Jesus was frequently unpopular with the religious establishment of his day because he dared to suggest that God's spirit might lead us to make changes. The focus of this sermon is the fact of change as part of the Christian life.

Experience: Something out of place in the church, together with the telling of the story of Jesus cleansing the Temple. You may or may not want to include a final experience of having the children return to a different seat somewhere in the church and then having their families come and join them, the purpose of which is to bring about change in the usually predictable seating, and thus interaction patterns, of people in a church.

Arrangements: The catalyst for this sermon is something that is noticeably out of place in the church. It may be a table, a chair, the cross, the baptismal font, the choir, and so forth, moved to a location that is clearly "wrong." Be sure ushers and others responsible for worship know not to move it back!

> **Leader:** Good morning! Will the children please meet me in the side aisle? *(As children assemble)* There's a change in the church today, what is it?
> **Children:** The cross!
> **L:** The cross is in the middle of the aisle! How do you suppose it got here?
> **C:** Don't know. Somebody moved it.
> **L:** Somebody has moved it. Do you think it's a change for the better; do you think that this is a good place for the cross to be?
> **C:** Yes. No.
> **L:** Well, before we decide on that, let me tell you a

story; some of you may already know it. One day
Jesus was in Jerusalem and decided to go into the
Temple. Inside there were people trading normal
money for a special kind of money you could only
use in the Temple, and other people were selling
things, and in general it was noisy and seemed more
like a store than a church. Do you know what Jesus
did?

C: He got mad.

L: He did get mad, and he made some changes! But
then some of the leaders in the Temple got mad at
Jesus, because they didn't want any changes. They
wanted things to be just the way they were. What do
you think, do you think God wants us to make
changes sometimes?

C: Yes. Maybe. Depends on if you're doing something
bad.

L: I think you're right. It seems that God wants us to
change if we're doing something bad, or if we could
just do something that's good even better. Well, what
about this cross? Do you think we should change it
back to where it was? Or do you think we should
leave it here as a reminder, at least for today, that
sometimes God wants us to make a change.

C: Leave it!

L: OK, well, let's have a prayer and thank God for
changes . . . *(prayer)*.

Brant D. Baker

Peter in Prison

Scripture: Acts 12:1-19

Season/Sunday: Any.

Focus: The story focuses on the amazing release of Peter and on the power of prayer to accomplish God's purposes even in the most desperate of circumstances.

Experience: This is an action story wherein the children will be invited to mimic a series of movements modeled by the leader (or a helper). If the children in the group are old enough (8–12 years), they could also echo the words as they follow the motion. For an additional option, ask the children to echo the last few words of each stanza. The leader can indicate which words by raising and lowering a hand, indicating the beginning and ending of the string of words. In the sermon below suggested words for this option are indicated in *italics*.

Arrangements: None.

> **Leader:** Good morning! Today we're going to hear an amazing story about a prison break. But it's no ordinary prison break. The prisoner didn't use a saw or a file or even dynamite to escape, but instead other people prayed him out! I'll say a few words and I'd like you to echo the words I say when my hand is raised. Then I'll do a motion and you copy me. Ready?
>
> **Children:** Ready!
>
> **L:** Peter kept proclaiming *the message of Jesus (cup hands around mouth)*
>
> **C:** . . . the message of Jesus *(copy motion)*.
>
> **L:** Until one day the rulers had him arrested and *put in prison (cross wrists to symbolize chains)*
>
> **C:** . . . put in prison *(copy motion)*.
>
> **L:** But his friends in the church *prayed for him (fold hands in prayer gesture)*

96

C: ... prayed for him *(copy motion)*.

L: *One night as he slept (place both hands on side of face and close eyes)*

C: One night as he slept *(copy motion)*

L: With prison *guards watching him (cup one hand over eyes)*

C: ... guards watching him *(copy motion)*,

L: Suddenly *an angel appeared (extend arms in gesture of surprise)*

C: ... an angel appeared *(copy motion)*.

L: *Peter's chains fell away (cross wrists and move arms down)*

C: Peter's chains fell away *(copy motion)*.

L: Peter and the angel walked *right past the guards (walk in place)*

C: ... right past the guards *(copy motion)*.

L: *In the cool night air (wrap arms around self)*

C: In the cool night air *(copy motion)*

L: Peter realized *he wasn't dreaming (place hands on cheeks in a gesture of surprise)*

C: ... he wasn't dreaming *(copy motion)*.

L: Peter walked to the house where *his friends met for church (walk in place)*

C: ... his friends met for church *(copy motion)*.

L: He knocked and *knocked on the door (knock)*

C: ... knocked on the door *(copy motion)*.

L: When Rhoda, the servant girl, *opened the door (gesture opening door)*

C: ... opened the door *(copy motion)*,

L: She was so surprised she slammed the door and *ran away (gesture slamming door and run in place)*

C: ... ran away *(copy motion)*.

L: *Peter knocked again (knock)*

C: Peter knocked again *(copy motion)*.

L: This time all his friends came to see *who was at the door (open door)*

C: ... who was at the door *(copy motion)*.

L: Imagine their *joy when they realized (cross hands over heart)*

C: ... joy when they realized *(copy motion)*

L: *Peter was truly free (extend arms wide)*
C: Peter was truly free *(copy motion).*
L: Isn't that a great story? Let's have a prayer right now for people we know who are imprisoned in pain, or sorrow, or poverty... *(prayer).*

Phyllis Wezeman

What Does God Do?

Scripture: Psalm 115:3

Season/Sunday: Any.

Focus: The freedom of God.

Experience: To imagine what God does and remember God is free to do anything.

Arrangements: None are needed, although a hand-held microphone to help amplify answers of children and others might be helpful.

Leader: Good morning. I have a question for you. What does God do? *(There may be a moment of silence, so ask again in another way.)* What do you think God does all day with all that time?

Children: God watches over us.

L: Great. Yes, God watches over us. What else does God do?

C: God gives us food.

L: Good. That's why we say thanks to God every time we eat. What else does God do?

C: God makes it rain.

L: That's right, God makes it rain.

C: God answers our prayers.

L: Yes, God does! Those are all great answers! I wonder what the adults think. Come with me while we throw the question to the congregation (move out into congregation, looking for volunteers). Mr. Abernathy, what does God do?

Adult: I think God takes care of us when we are in need.

L: That's a good answer (moving on to next adult). Justine, what do you think God does?

Adult: I think God is loving us all the time.

L: Wow, good answer. Let's see, one more: Chris, what does God do all day long?

Adult: Well, the Bible says that Jesus prays for us...

L: That's right, that's good too! Thank you all for helping. There's one more answer that comes from Psalm
115:3, "Our God is in the heavens; / he does whatever he pleases." Hmmm! So next time someone asks
you what God does, just say, whatever God wants
to. Let's have a prayer and give thanks that what
God seems mostly to want to do is to love and take
care of us... *(prayer).*

Jeff Hutcheson

The Body of Christ

Scripture: Romans 12:4-5; 1 Corinthians 12:14-26; Ephesians 4:14-16

Season/Sunday: Any, but sometime around stewardship season might work well.

Focus: The Body of Christ is Paul's powerful image to describe the interrelated structure of the church. Each part needs the other; each part has a specific task that it is uniquely able to perform. The focus of this sermon is to explore what these different parts of the Body are in a particular church.

Experience: To relate the parts of the body mentioned by Paul to specific groups within the church, by asking members of those groups to stand when they hear their group called (and its corresponding part in the body you have assigned to it). Children will be asked to stand when they see their parents stand to form bridges from parent to child through church service groups.

Arrangements: You will need a list of the various parts of the body mentioned by Paul in 1 Corinthians, alongside a list of all the groups in your church. Organize the list to match your church's ministries. The list shown here is an example.

> **Leader:** Good to see you today! I want to read to you a few verses from the Bible, from the book of Romans. "As in one body we have many members, and not all the members have the same function, so we, who are many, are one body in Christ, and individually we are members one of another." A man named Paul wrote these words, and he is saying that a church is a lot like our body. Part of the church is a foot, part of it is a hand, part of it is an eye. Do you know which parts of our church are these things?
>
> **Children:** No.
>
> **L:** I thought you might not, so I made a list! *(To the*

101

congregation) How about standing when I call out a part of our church body that you're a member of? *(To children)* And how about standing when you see your folks stand, OK? Then here we go.

- Foot   Missions Ministry
- Hand   Deacons or Trustees
- Ear   Women's Circle or Youth Ministry
- Eye   Worship Leaders and Planners
- Arm   Sunday school classes
- Elbow   Christian Education

(And so on; your list can be as brief or as compre- hensive as you like! It probably would be good, however, to end with the following:) And now, will *all* of the other parts of this Body of Christ please stand?

   (To the children) There's one very important part of the body that I didn't mention, the head. Who do you suppose is the head of the church?

C: The minister? My daddy? Jesus?

L: Some interesting answers, but I think I'd have to agree that Jesus is the head of the church! Jesus is the one who tells all of the other parts what to do, and then helps them do what they need to do.

   Let's have a prayer, and since we're all standing up, let's all hold hands while we thank God that we are joined together in one Body, with Jesus Christ as our head . . . *(prayer)*.

Brant D. Baker

Give of Your Best to the Master

Scripture: Mark 14:3-9 (NIV)

Season/Sunday: Stewardship.

Focus: Giving our best in whatever we do.

Experience: Children will be reminded of the many gifts they have to offer to the work of Christ.

Arrangements: Arrange with the musician and choir to play and sing the first stanza of "Give of Your Best to the Master" at the close of the story (Howard B. Grose and Charlotte A. Barnard, *Worship & Service Hymnal*, Hope Publishing Co., Carol Stream, IL). Also, having a bottle of nice-smelling perfume for the children to smell will help engage other senses (but be cautious of actually spraying, as some people may be allergic!).

> **Leader:** Who can remember being in a department store perfume section? (*Wait for a show of hands*) What comes to mind when you think about the perfume counters?
>
> **Children:** (*Various responses*)
>
> **L:** In the ancient world, when Jesus lived, perfume was very valuable and not everyone was able to buy it. But in the Bible we read a story about a woman who managed to come by a bottle of very expensive perfume, a bottle that would have lasted her probably months or years, even. Well, one day, while Jesus was having dinner at a friend's house, this woman came in, walked up behind Jesus, and then poured this very expensive, sweet-smelling perfume on Jesus' head. Well, when everyone saw what had happened, some of them got angry. And they said, "What a waste!" And they started saying cruel things to the woman, which hurt her feelings (as you can imagine). Jesus stepped in and he said, "Leave her alone!

... She has done a beautiful thing for me." Then Jesus said, "She gave the best she had to give" (from Mark 14:6-8). Can you say that with me?

L & C: She gave the best she had to give!

L: Good! You know, what we have to give to the work of Jesus may not be perfume, like the woman in the story. But we have many other things that we can give, don't we? And when we give, we can give the best we have to give. Say that with me.

L & C: We can give the best we have to give.

L: When we give an offering of money, instead of giving nothing *(prompt children for response, and so on throughout)*,

C: We can give the best we have to give.

L: When we sing in children's choir, instead of complaining about rehearsals,

C: We can give the best we have to give.

L: When we help straighten up the classroom at the end of class, instead of moaning,

C: We can give the best we have to give.

L: When it's time to say our prayers, instead of grumbling about being too tired,

C: We can give the best we have to give.

L: That was great! Let's have a prayer and give thanks that God gives us many good gifts to share and asks us to always give our best in whatever we do ... *(prayer)*. Since we mentioned giving our best when we sing, our choir is going to sing the first stanza of "Give of Your Best to the Master" (or alternative) as you return to your seats.

Randy Hammer

A Cloud of Witnesses

Scripture: Hebrews 12:1

Season/Sunday: All Saints Day.

Focus: The Christian heritage that we have, reaching back into the Jewish faith.

Experience: The children will choose a color in a fabric to represent biblical characters. The congregation will help the children respond to descriptions of persons in our faith heritage.

Arrangements: A piece of fabric with as many colors as possible, preferably a fabric where the colors are woven, and a Bible.

Leader:	Good morning! Does anyone know what's special about today?
Children:	*(Various responses)*
L:	Today is All Saints Day. And just what is a saint?
C:	*(Various responses)*
L:	In the church, we call those who love God and try to follow God a saint. Do you love God and try to follow God?
C:	Yes!
L:	Then you are all saints! This piece of fabric has many colors in it. We are going to choose one color to represent different people in our faith heritage. A heritage is what people of the past have given us. Which of these colors is a favorite of yours?
C:	*(Various responses)*
L:	*(Lifting up the Bible)* There were many people in the past who have loved God. We could say that these people are a part of our heritage. Their stories help us know how to live, so their stories are the heritage, or gift, to us. The Bible tells us about some of these people. What are the names of some of the people you remember from the Bible?

105

C: *(Various responses)*

L: I'm going to tell you briefly about several different people, and I want you to respond with the person's name. We'll ask the congregation to help us too. When I say, "and his (or her) name is...," if you remember the story you will shout out the name. Congregation, you be sure to shout the names too! Are you ready?

C: Yes!

L: There was a man that God told to go to a faraway land to live. He and his wife were very old, but they had no children. God told this man that they would have a son, and their son would have many children, and their children would have many children—as many as the stars in the sky. That man was a saint and a part of our heritage, and his name was... *(point to children and congregation for the response)*.

C: Abraham!

L: And his wife's name was...

C: Sarah!

L: Remember, I said that these people are a part of our heritage. Let's choose two colors in the fabric, one for Abraham and one for Sarah *(if fabric has too few colors, feel free to assign both Abraham and Sarah one color, and so on throughout)*.

C: *(Offer suggestions and decide on two colors.)*

L: Much later God's people were slaves in Egypt, and the ruler tried to kill all of the boy babies, but one woman put her baby into a basket and floated it in a river where the ruler's daughter would find him. When the baby was grown, God told him to help the people get away from the cruel ruler. God even helped them by making a path for them to go through the sea and seeing that they had food, or manna, in the wilderness. The leader that God chose to help the people get away was named... *(point to children and congregation for response)*.

C: Moses!

L: Moses had a sister who watched over him when he

was a baby and later helped him lead the people.
Her name was...

C: Miriam!

L: Let's choose two more colors in the fabric, one for
Moses and one for Miriam.

C: *(Offer suggestions and decide on two colors.)*

L: There was a young man who killed a giant of a man
with a sling and a rock. Later he became a king who
ruled the Hebrew people well. The name of this king
was...

C: David!

L: Let's choose a color in the fabric for David.

C: *(Decide on a color for David.)*

L: Two thousand years ago a baby was born in a stable.
He grew up to be a teacher and a healer who helped
many people and told us how to live together peacefully. Some rulers did not understand what he was
telling the people and put him to death on a cross,
but God would not let him stay dead. This special
man was called...

C: Jesus!

L: Let's choose a color in the fabric for Jesus.

C: *(Decide on a color for Jesus.)*

L: There were many others after Jesus who helped us
understand God. You may have heard of them.
There were Paul and Barnabas, mentioned in the
Bible. And later on there were other leaders, some of
them are even called saints, like Saint Francis and
Saint Teresa. You may have heard of Martin Luther
and John Wesley. There were people who helped to
start this very church many years ago. Some of them
were *(mention the names of some of your church
founders)*.

   All of these people are like this multi-colored
fabric. Let's all take hold of the fabric and think
of the people who were a part of the past. Let's
have a prayer and thank God for all these
people... *(prayer)*.

Delia Halverson

A Highway for God

Scripture: Isaiah 40:3

Season/Sunday: Advent.

Focus: The sermon focuses on some of the things we can do to get ready for Jesus' coming.

Experience: The children will experience an interruption in the form of workers trying to build a highway through the church to "prepare the way of the Lord," and will be asked to come up with some alternative ideas for getting ready.

Arrangements: You will need at least three helpers: two workers and one supervisor. Instruct them to wear a tool belt with tape measures and other tools. The supervisor may want to carry a roll of plans and should also have a Bible. It would be fun if they had orange vests or hard hats.

Leader:	Good morning! How is everyone this morning?
Children:	Good!
Supervisor:	*(Loudly entering sanctuary)* OK, Bob, you and Sharon measure the pew here, and I'll start laying out the blueprints *(workers start activities)*.
L:	*(Inviting children to follow, move toward one of the workers)* Excuse me. What are you doing?
Worker 1:	Sorry, I don't have time to talk right now. I'm busy getting ready *(continues working and measuring)*.
L:	*(Invite children to follow as you approach next worker, interacting with them as you go about how sorry you are, how unbelievable this is, and so forth)* Excuse me, but I'm trying to have a children's sermon here. What are you doing?
Worker 2:	Look, I just go where they tell me. But we don't have much time. We have to get this highway finished.
L:	*(Shocked)* Highway?!
Worker 2:	*(Distracted and busy)* That's what I said.

L: Here?

Worker 2: Yep.

L: You can't build a highway here. There must be some mistake!

Worker 2: I've really got to get this job finished. We don't have much time. *(Pointing)* Ask him your questions; he's the supervisor.

L: *(Inviting children to follow as you approach last worker)* Are you the supervisor?

Supervisor: I sure am. What can I do for you?

L: You can't build a highway here. This is a sanctuary.

Supervisor: Not for long.

L: Who told you to build this highway?

Supervisor: *(Hands leader an open Bible)* Got my building permit right here.

L: *(Reading)* "In the wilderness prepare the way of the LORD, make straight in the desert a highway for our God" (Isaiah 40:3). Oh, I see.

Supervisor: This is Advent. It's time to get ready for the coming of the Lord.

L: Well, you're right about that, but maybe there are some other ways we could do that. *(Addressing the children)* Quick, can you help me think of some other ways we prepare for the coming of the Lord?

C: Decorating, cleaning up, praying, being nice...

L: Those are some great ideas! *(Addressing supervisors)* What do you think? Could we prepare by doing those things rather than by building a highway?

Supervisor: *(Showing some disappointment)* Well, I suppose so. All right, crew, let's wrap it up here *(workers collect tools and leave)*.

L: Wow, thanks so much for coming up with those good ideas, and let's keep doing those things—praying, being nice, cleaning up—so that we're ready to welcome the Lord again this Christmas! Let's have a prayer and give thanks that we have this time to prepare... *(prayer)*.

Jeff Hutcheson

Evergreen!

Scripture: John 3:16

Season/Sunday: Advent/Christmas.

Focus: To understand that evergreen is a symbol of eternal life.

Experience: Children will pass out sprigs of evergreen to the congregation.

Arrangements: Cut branches of evergreen such as boxwood or pine. Trim into small sprigs three to six inches in length. The evergreen will stay fresh much longer if you soak it in water for a day or two. Dry on paper towels and place the sprigs in one or several baskets. At the end of the sermon, the children will pass out evergreen to the congregation. If your congregation is quite large, this may be impractical. In this case, you can invite the children to pass out a sprig to just one other person.

Leader: *(Hold up an evergreen sprig.)* What's this?
Children: Evergreen. A plant. Boxwood. A pine sprig.
L: This is *(say the kind of evergreen)*. It's an evergreen. What does it mean if something is "ever green"?
C: It's always green. It doesn't turn brown and die.
L: An evergreen is a plant that stays green all year long, as long as it's planted and watered. It even stays green for a long time after you take it out of the ground. During the Christmas season, we decorate our church and our home with evergreen *(point out any evergreen in your sanctuary)*. We do this because evergreen is a symbol of eternal life. There's a Bible verse that says: "For God so loved the world that he gave his only Son, so that everyone who believes in him may not perish but may have eternal life." Since Jesus was born at Christmas, we celebrate this gift of eternal life by decorating with evergreen. Just as the evergreen doesn't die back in the winter, God prom-

ises eternal life to those who believe in Jesus. Say
after me, "Evergreen is a symbol of eternal life."

C: Evergreen is a symbol of eternal life.

L: Now let's share some of this wonderful evergreen
with the rest of the congregation! *(Invite the children
to pass out sprigs of the evergreen. Keep enough
sprigs with you so the children can each have
one. When they have finished handing out the
evergreen, call them forward again and give them
each a sprig.)* Let's say a prayer thanking God for
Jesus, eternal life, and the Christmas symbol of evergreen... *(prayer)*.

Barbara Younger

The Season of Hope

Scripture: Mark 13:28-29

Season/Sunday: Advent.

Focus: The focus of this sermon is to emphasize the signs of hope all around us.

Experience: The children will identify objects in the sanctuary that are not usually there, as a way of identifying signs that Christmas is on the way.

Arrangements: Assuming the sanctuary is already decorated for Advent, the leader will need to know the importance of each of the various symbols (see below). The leader could add additional objects that are more common to secular settings, such as reindeer, a Christmas tree, sleigh bells, or Santa. Some thought should be given to contemporary signs of hope in the congregation or community to include in the leader's closing remarks.

> **Leader:** Good morning, everyone. I'm glad to see you! Did you know that the four Sundays leading up to Christmas each have a special theme? One of those is the word *hope*. What does it mean to hope?
>
> **Children:** *(Various replies)*
>
> **L:** Those are some good answers to a word that is kind of hard to understand. To me hope means the feeling I get when I know that sooner or later something good is going to happen. And today in our sanctuary we have a lot of signs to remind us that something good is going to happen, some things that are not usually here. What do you see that is not usually here and reminds you of something good?
>
> **C:** I see a Christmas tree!
>
> **L:** Yup, there's a tree. We use evergreen trees and holly and greenery to decorate our sanctuary for the celebration of Jesus' birth. Because they are some of the few plants that are green in the middle of winter, they give us hope. What else do you see?

C: I see some candles.

L: Yes, we call that the Advent wreath. These four weeks before Christmas are known as the season of Advent, and they are a time to prepare our hearts for the coming of Jesus. The Advent wreath helps us count down the four Sundays leading up to Christmas day, and we use candles to give us hope in Jesus, the light of the world. What else do you see?

C: I see Santa!

L: Yes, we don't usually have Santa in the sanctuary, but I added him today because he is part of the season of hope too. Santa's real name is St. Nicholas, who long ago came to poor children in the night and left surprises for them. You're doing so well! What else do you see?

C: I see a manger with the baby Jesus.

L: I love our church manger! The manger scene is sometimes called the crèche and reminds us of the very plain place that Jesus was born. He wasn't born in a fancy castle, but in a stable for animals. But no matter where he was born, the fact is that he came to earth and that gives us the most hope of all! Now what do all these signs or things make you think of?

C: Christmas!

L: Yes, Christmas. They are all signs that something good is coming, and that something good is Christmas. Can I tell you some other things that give me hope? *(Leader should adapt the following to his or her own setting.)* When one of you brought your whole piggy bank in and gave it to the church to give to Heifer Project to help other people, that gave me hope. When one of our youth broke something at camp by accident and didn't try and hide it but took responsibility, that gave me hope. Every Sunday when you come down here and kneel and make room for new people to kneel next to you, that gives me hope. And on a rainy day like today, when I see your smiling faces here at church, I feel hope!

Let's have a prayer and give thanks for all of the hope God is giving us... *(prayer)*.

Karen Evans

Gifts to Give

Scripture: Romans 12:6-8; 1 Corinthians 12:8-11; Galatians 5:22

Season/Sunday: Any, especially appropriate for a Sunday near Christmas.

Focus: God has given us gifts, and we share our gifts with others.

Experience: The children will become excited over gift-wrapped packages and open a gift to reveal a way that they can give gifts to others.

Arrangements: Enough wrapped gifts for each child to have a choice, leaving no child to receive "the last one." Inside each gift box will be a slip of paper with one of the following words on them: love, friendship, joy, happiness, cooperation, goodness, kindness, sharing. Have a trash basket or some other receptacle for the paper litter.

Leader: Good morning! Did you ever see so many gifts? I had to really work to get all these gifts wrapped! Do you like to wrap gifts?

Children: *(Varied responses)*

L: What do you suppose is in all these gifts?

C: *(Varied responses)*

L: Do you know that God has given us all gifts? God gave the men and women in our choir beautiful voices. God gave your parents arms to hug you. God gave us all trees and flowers. God gave us colors. What do you suppose the world would have been like without color?

C: *(Varied responses)*

L: God could have made the world in black and white, and we'd never have known about color! God gave you *(point to a child who is smiling)* a big smile! In these boxes you will find a word that tells us about a gift that God gave us that we can give to someone else. You may each unwrap a gift, and we will see what gifts we have that we can share with others.

C: *(Unwrap gifts.)*

L: Now, perhaps some of you who can read will help those children who can't read yet. (*If you have many non-readers, encourage adults nearby to help.*) Who has the word LOVE?

C: *(Responses from those with the word.)*

L: Remember, I said that these are gifts that God has given us that we can share with others. What is a way that we can share love with others?

C: *(Varied responses; acknowledge each.)*

L: Who has the word FRIENDSHIP? (*Continue with each of the words, or until every child has shared his or her word.*)

C: *(Varied responses; acknowledge each.)*

L: You may take your word gift home and find ways this week to share that gift with people in your family, people in your school, and even people you don't know. Let's have a prayer to thank God for all of our gifts . . . (*prayer*).

Delia Halverson

Contributors

Brant D. Baker holds graduate degrees from Princeton Theological Seminary and Columbia Theological Seminary. He served churches in the southern United States prior to becoming senior pastor of First Presbyterian Church in Mesa, Arizona. Dr. Baker has written numerous books, including three on children's sermons. Two of his titles, *Play That Preaches* and *Teaching P.R.A.Y.E.R.,* are available from Abingdon Press. Brant is married and has two teenagers.

Karen Evans is the Minister of Spiritual Formation and Family Ministries at First United Methodist Church in Pensacola, Florida, where she has served for nineteen years. Karen is a graduate of Huntingdon College and Duke Divinity School. She also has a Specialist degree in Education from the University of Florida. Karen is an ordained deacon in The United Methodist Church, a certified Christian Educator, and a spiritual director. Karen is married and has two teenage children. Her passions include children and youth, stories, Duke basketball, and walking the spiritual journey with others.

Joyce Fong is a special education teacher in New York City, teaching children with emotional disturbance in kindergarten through second grade. She has a master of arts in Christian education from Union Theological Seminary and Presbyterian School of Christian Education. Her focal interest is in children's ministry, and she has assumed varied roles, such as children's worship director, Sunday school teacher, and day camp co-director.

Delia Halverson is an internationally known Christian education consultant, workshop leader, and keynote speaker. She has authored twenty books including *The Nuts and Bolts of Christian Education, 32 Ways to Become a Great Sunday*

School Teacher, Side by Side: Families Learning and Living in Faith Together, and *Growing the Soul: Meditations from My Garden.* Delia and her husband have lived across the U.S., and currently reside in Georgia.

Randy Hammer is pastor of First Congregational Church, United Church of Christ, of Albany, New York. He holds a master of divinity from Memphis Theological Seminary and a doctor of divinity from Meadville Lombard Theological School. Other published works include *Dancing in the Dark: Lessons in Facing Life's Challenges with Courage and Creativity* (Pilgrim Press, 1998) and *Everyone A Butterfly: Forty Sermons for Children* (Skinner House, 2004).

Jeff L. Hutcheson is pastor of the First Presbyterian Church of Cleveland, Georgia. He has also served congregations in Florida and Alabama. Jeff received a master of divinity from Columbia Theological Seminary, and also holds a master in psychology from Auburn University at Montgomery, Alabama. He continues to be an aspiring writer and is currently completing a Ph.D. in Human and Organizational Development. He lives in the "gateway to the mountains" with his wife, Sherry, and their two dogs, Chewy and Gizmo.

Susan M. Lang is a church consultant and pastor in the Evangelical Lutheran Church in America. She is the author of several books, including: *Our Community: Dealing with Conflict in Our Congregation* (Augsburg Fortress, 2002) and *Welcome Forward: A Field Guide for Global Travelers,* co-authored with Rochelle Melander (ELCA, 2005). She publishes the RevWriter Resource, a free electronic newsletter for busy church leaders (www.revwriter.com).

Ann Liechty is a National Board Certified teacher and chair of the English Department at Plymouth High School in Indiana. She has worked as a religious education volunteer, teacher, consultant, and youth programming director. She has consulted with congregations about their educational ministry and has written a wide variety of religious education materials. Ann lives in Plymouth, Indiana, with her husband, Ron, a retired pastor. They have five children, ten grandchildren, and a great-grandson.

William Robert (Bob) Sharman III, a Presbyterian minister, has served churches in Alabama and Germany, where he served the American Protestant Church of Bonn. He presently serves as senior minister at Jamestown Presbyterian Church in Jamestown, North Carolina, and thanks the Children's Sermon Leaders at Jamestown Presbyterian for their ideas, enthusiasm, and effort. A graduate of the University of Mississippi, Princeton Theological Seminary, and Columbia Theological Seminary, Bob is married and has three children and a golden retriever.

Phyllis Wezeman is President of Active Learning Associates, Inc. and Director of Christian Nurture at First Presbyterian Church in South Bend, Indiana. Phyllis has served as adjunct faculty in education in various settings and has taught in Russia and China. Phyllis, who holds a master of science in education from Indiana University, is a recipient of three "Distinguished Alumni Awards." She is widely published and with her husband, Ken, has three children and three grandsons.

Barbara Younger, along with her friend Lisa Flinn, is the author of more than fifteen books for Abingdon Press including *Mystery in the Stable, Unwrapping the Christmas Creche*, and *Celebrating God's World in Children's Church*. She is presently studying for a master of fine Arts in Writing for Children and Young Adults. Barbara has two grown daughters and lives in Hillsborough, North Carolina, with her husband and her cat, Lillian.

Scripture Index